Horoscope 2023

....

Pisces

20 February – 20 March

igloobooks

igloobooks

Published in 2022
First published in the UK by Igloo Books Ltd
An imprint of Igloo Books Ltd
Cottage Farm, NN6 0BJ, UK
Owned by Bonnier Books
Sveavägen 56, Stockholm, Sweden
www.igloobooks.com

Copyright © 2022 Igloo Books Ltd

0722 001
2 4 6 8 10 9 7 5 3 1
ISBN 978-1-80108-404-8

Written by Sally Kirkman
Additional content by Belinda Campbell and Denise Evans

Cover designed by Richard Sykes
Interiors designed by Chris Stanley
Edited by Luke Robertson

Printed and manufactured in China

CONTENTS

. . . .

INTRODUCTION
· · · · · · · · · · · · · · · · · ·

This 15-month guide has been designed and written to give a concise and accessible insight into both the nature of your star sign and the year ahead. Divided into two main sections, the first part of this guide will give you an overview of your character in order to help you understand how you think, perceive the world and interact with others and – perhaps just as importantly – why. You'll soon see that your zodiac sign is not just affected by a few stars in the sky, but by planets, elements and a whole host of other factors, too.

The second part of this guide is made up of daily forecasts. Use these to increase your awareness of what might appear on your horizon so that you're better equipped to deal with the days ahead. While this should never be used to dictate your life, it can be useful to see how your energies might be affected or influenced, which in turn can help you prepare for what life might throw your way.

By the end of these 15 months, these two sections should have given you a deeper understanding and awareness of yourself and, in turn, the world around you. There are never any certainties in life, but with an open mind you will find guidance for what might be, and learn to take more control of your own destiny.

THE CHARACTER OF THE TWO FISH

· · · · · · · · · · · · · · · · ·

Compassionate, creative and charitable, Pisceans are the visionary dreamers who breathe magic into the world. Whether they're illusionists like Derren Brown or storytellers like Dr. Seuss, the enchanting Pisces bring joy and expand the minds of others. Neptune and Jupiter co-rule Pisces, providing this sign with a limitless imagination and a thirst for growth. At times, Pisceans can get lost in their fantasies and become detached from reality, but a helping hand of support and encouragement from their friends and family will soon bring a lost Pisces back to reality. Wherever a Piscean's passion lies, however, their imagination will shine through. Examples include Paul Hollywood's baking, Michelangelo's Sistine Chapel and even Albert Einstein's Theory of Relativity.

A Piscean's negative energy means that they are often more focused on their internal growth than on experiencing external stimuli. This means that mental, spiritual and emotional journeys are those that this sign enjoys the most. The Two Fish that symbolise this sign hint at a dual and slippery nature that makes this elusive shapeshifter of the sea hard to pin down. As a water sign governed by their emotions, they may sometimes get carried away on a fast-moving current, so should be careful not to drown their loved ones in their overwhelming excitement. Belonging to the twelfth house of the zodiac, where sacrifice and devotion are key, there is surely no sign that is more generous with their time and love than pious Pisces. However, this sign should be careful that their self-sacrificing tendencies don't turn them into a martyr, as Pisceans can have a reputation for sometimes playing the victim. As the snow begins to melt and the daffodils bloom, mutable Pisceans are born, and bring with them a wise understanding of what has come before. Born at the end of both winter and the zodiac calendar, Pisceans are often the most adaptable and understanding of all the signs, having learned something from each of the star signs before them.

THE TWO FISH

Symbolised by the Two Fish, Pisces is one of the signs of the zodiac calendar with a dual symbol. The duality of Pisces suggests flexibility in their emotions, and getting excited for a project one day before becoming bored with it the next will be all too familiar to many Pisceans. However, as the last of the water signs, the Two Fish of Pisces are capable of exploring the true depth of their emotions, encompassing both the allure of seductive Scorpio and sensitivity of family-orientated Cancer. These slippery Fish try to wriggle their way out of even the tightest of spots by coming up with the most fantastical fibs. However, if a reluctant Piscean constantly swims away from the truth, they may end up going in circles, chasing their own tales just as the Two Fish in their symbol chase each other's tails. This sign should try to remember that, by accepting their slip-ups, they can then learn important lessons and avoid making the same mistakes in the future.

JUPITER AND NEPTUNE

Co-ruled by both the largest planet in the sky, Jupiter, and imaginative Neptune, Pisceans are certainly big dreamers. Jupiter, the ruler of the gods in Roman mythology, governed over the sky while his brother Neptune ruled the seas, and this is why Pisceans are a double force to be reckoned with. At times, dreamy Pisceans may have their heads stuck in their Jupiter clouds, while in other moments their feelings are as deep as Neptune's waters and as elusive and mythical as a mermaid. Jupiter is the fastest spinning planet in the solar system, which means that it has the shortest days of all the planets. As such, a tardy Piscean might be quick to blame their sign for their lateness. Pisceans can be incredibly understanding, but when pushed too far, their anger can be as tempestuous as the sea. Neptune is associated with spiritual intuition, and its rule helps guide this compassionate water sign to better understand the world, while adventurous Jupiter helps them explore and find their place within it.

ELEMENTS, MODES AND POLARITIES

Each sign is made up of a unique combination of three defining groups: elements, modes and polarities. Each of these defining parts can manifest themselves in good and bad ways, and none should be seen as a positive or a negative – including the polarities! Just like a jigsaw puzzle, piecing these groups together can help illuminate why each sign has certain characteristics and help us find a balance.

ELEMENTS

Fire: Dynamic and adventurous, signs with fire in them are often extroverted. Others are naturally drawn to them because of the positive light they give off, as well as their high levels of energy and confidence.

Earth: Signs with the earth element are steady and driven. They make for solid friends, parents and partners due to their grounded influence and nurturing nature.

Air: The invisible element that influences each of the other elements significantly, air signs provide much-needed perspective to those around them with their fair thinking, verbal skills and key ideas.

Water: Warm in the shallows but sometimes freezing as ice, the emotional depth and empathy of this mysterious element is essential to the growth of everything around it.

MODES

Cardinal: Pioneers of the calendar, cardinal signs jump-start each season and are the energetic go-getters.

Fixed: Marking the middle of the calendar, fixed signs firmly denote and value both steadiness and reliability.

Mutable: As the seasons end, the mutable signs adapt and gladly give themselves over to the promise of change.

POLARITIES

Positive: Typically extroverted, positive signs take physical action and embrace external stimulus in their life.

Negative: Usually introverted, negative signs value emotional development and experiencing life from the inside out.

PISCES IN BRIEF

The table below shows the key attributes of Pisceans.
Use it for quick reference and to understand more about this fascinating sign.

SYMBOL	RULING PLANETS	MODE	ELEMENT	HOUSE
Two Fish	Jupiter and Neptune	Mutable	Water	Twelfth

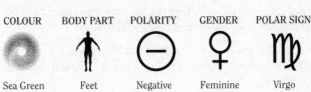

COLOUR	BODY PART	POLARITY	GENDER	POLAR SIGN
Sea Green	Feet	Negative	Feminine	Virgo

ROMANTIC RELATIONSHIPS

· · · · · · · · · · · · · · · · ·

Pisceans are the romantics of the zodiac and will no doubt fantasise about being swept off their feet, just like the starry-eyed characters from their favourite romance novels and films. Their intoxicating imagination and endless generosity rarely fail to charm, so they are not likely to be short of admirers. As a mutable and self-sacrificing sign, overly generous Pisceans are sometimes at risk of being too agreeable. Pisces should try to avoid being passengers in their relationships, and should instead take an active role in their love life. Sitting in the driving seat and taking on more responsibilities, whether it's choosing a restaurant for dinner or sorting out the home insurance, will boost an unsure Piscean's self-confidence and give their partner a break from constant decision-making.

As a mutable water sign, Pisceans are highly intuitive lovers that adapt to their partner's emotional needs. They often crave change, which can cause this sign to flip between their emotions and struggle to bind to just the one lover. Symbolised by not one but two fish, Pisces is a dual sign that is prone to going back and forth, changing their mind and feelings. While the Two Fish are deciding on a partner who is best suited to them, they may have a few contenders in the running. This can hurt their potential partners, especially if there is any deceit going on. If this sign can stick to the truth, they stand a chance of staying out of hot water with their lovers. Under the philosophical influence of Jupiter and the spiritualism of Neptune, an easy-going Piscean will likely have a relaxed attitude when it comes to being with someone or not, and might be happy to leave it up to the universe to decide for them.

ARIES: COMPATIBILITY 2/5

Dreamy Pisces and action-loving Aries can learn a lot from each other. Watery Pisces may fear delving into the deep end of their desires and prefer to stay in the warmer, shallower waters of their comfort zone, generally choosing to emotionally support their partners' dreams over their own. Aries, on the other hand, will want to help Pisces reach their full potential, but should be wary of offending this water sign, as Pisces is known to overflow with emotions when pushed too far. If Pisces can offer much-needed emotional support to Aries, the two will form a thoughtful connection that is deeper than most.

TAURUS: COMPATIBILITY 3/5

Taurus and Pisces are capable of sharing a highly sympathetic and understanding love. The practically minded Taurus should encourage the dreamy Pisces to live out their fantasies and work hard for themselves, not just others. In return, a Piscean will shower their Taurus in waves of love and gratitude for helping them realise their dreams. However, a Piscean would be wise not to emotionally saturate the relationship or otherwise spoil a Taurus. As Pisces is a water sign, Taureans will feel the nourishing effects in their earth element, and this will help the pair grow a life worth living together.

GEMINI: COMPATIBILITY 3/5

As fluid as water and free flowing as air, Pisces and Gemini may experience an extremely flexible and forgiving relationship if they fall for each other. Both mutable signs, this couple has the potential to be highly compatible. They won't fight for leadership, and will instead rule side by side. Even if these two don't always understand each other, their open-minded attitudes will help resolve their disagreements. While Gemini is led by the mind influence of Mercury, the Piscean's influence of water means that they are often ruled by their emotions. A meeting of the head and heart will be key.

CANCER: COMPATIBILITY 4/5

These two feminine water signs can be a vision of romance together. A Cancerian is well placed to identify with the changeable river of emotion that runs within Pisces, because the same river runs within them too. These are two signs that enjoy nurturing their loved ones, and this means their love will be built on a mutual support system. Be mindful not to drown in the floods of emotions that both the Crab and Fish are capable of unleashing in their romantic relationships, and instead try to let love and compassion flow gently.

LEO: COMPATIBILITY 2/5

When Leo meets Pisces, each can bring out the best and worst in each other. Pisces will be a source of emotional encouragement for Leo, while Leo may help the dreamy Pisces take more action in their life, helping both to realise their dreams. Born in the twelfth house, which represents sacrifice, Pisces is selfless, while Leo's Sun influence means that they can often be selfish. When these sacrificing and self-serving characteristics are felt at their extremes, things can quickly turn sour. However, mutable Pisces and fixed Leo can live in harmony if they both value each other's best qualities.

VIRGO: COMPATIBILITY 5/5

Opposites on the zodiac calendar, hands-on Virgo and mystical Pisces can be a loving match, but will not be without their struggles. The slippery fish symbol of Pisces can hint at an elusiveness that can be both attractive and frustrating to steady earth sign Virgo. While water and earth are elements that can create beautiful things together, the emotional Piscean and rational Virgo could prove to be a tricky balancing act. These two are deep souls that have the potential to empathise and support one another better than any other sign pairing.

LIBRA: COMPATIBILITY 1/5

While the enigmatic Pisces and suave Libra might be charmed by each other, theirs is a love that will struggle to come to fruition. Cardinal Libras are more likely to be the initiator in a relationship with mutable Pisceans, but both signs may be struck with an inability to make decisions, leaving them both treading water. Libras will be attracted to the artistic side of the creative Piscean, while Pisceans are likely to flourish as a result of encouragement from their positive Libra partner. If the pair can find a balance between Libra's extroverted nature and Piscean's introverted nature, their romance will bloom.

SCORPIO: COMPATIBILITY 4/5

Here are two water signs that will go to the ends of the Earth, or even the depths of the oceans, for one another. Pisceans dream of finding their fantasy love, and the enigmatic Scorpio can be just that. Similarly, Pisces can be the kindred spirit that secretive Scorpios are finally able to be vulnerable around. A Piscean's mutable nature, which flows with change, may be at odds with the steadfast approach of a fixed Scorpio, but their differences mean that they have plenty to learn from each other. Emotional security and sensitivity are areas where these two thrive.

SAGITTARIUS: COMPATIBILITY 3/5

The roaming Sagittarius and the escapist Pisces will end up blissfully running off into the sunset together if they can learn from each other's differences. Both ruled by lucky Jupiter, these two may indeed have been fortunate to find one another. Jupiter gives Sagittarians and Pisceans a zest for life, and their shared mutable modes will help this relationship to grow and change. Pisceans often lack the active side that many fire signs have, while Sagittarians' lack of compassion might clash with this sensitive water sign. If they focus on common interests, this deep pair could go far.

CAPRICORN: COMPATIBILITY 3/5

An earth and water love is bound to be a complementary match, and the relationship between a Capricorn and Piscean will likely be about helping each other grow as individuals and flourish as a couple. Capricorn brings a practical mind and an active spirit to a relationship, while the mutable Piscean provides compassion and will teach their Goat to be flexible. Both sides can retreat into themselves at times of great focus or reflection, particularly if one half of this couple is being overbearing. However, their matching negative energies have the potential to form a deep emotional connection that could make for a special relationship.

AQUARIUS: COMPATIBILITY 2/5

Two sharing signs such as Pisces and Aquarius could happily give themselves to each other in love. While an air and water sign may struggle to understand one another, the combination of an Aquarian's intellect and Piscean's compassion may form a relationship that speaks to both the heart and head, especially if flexibility and patience are practised by the pair. This fixed and mutable pairing can be a complementary match, so long as Aquarians don't try to bend the will of their accommodating Piscean partner. At its best, the bond that these two can share will be sincere and spiritually liberating.

PISCES: COMPATIBILITY 2/5

Two Pisceans might easily capture each other's hearts and imaginations, but their easy-going mutable nature might mean that their feelings for one another struggle to gain traction, making it hard for them to form a solid relationship. However, once these two (or four) Fish decide to commit, their love can be full of thoughtful gift giving and deep emotional understanding. These two water signs' positive and negative energies can make them sponge-like, and this could bring out the best or worst both of them, depending on what they offer to the relationship.

FAMILY AND FRIENDS

· · · · · · · · · · · · · · · · ·

As a water sign, Pisceans are incredibly attuned to the needs of their family and friends and can pick up on even the slightest of changes in their loved ones' emotions. A caring Piscean will not think twice about dropping what they are doing to go to a friend's aid, as is their self-sacrificing way. The kind words of a Piscean can help heal many emotional wounds, and they will often know just what to say, much to the relief of their family and friends. This eternally compassionate sign is only too glad to give themselves to others that need their support. Kindred spirits for Pisceans are the friends and family that reciprocate their support and encouragement. Fellow water sign Cancer has the potential to be a strong ally, because their emotional sensitivity and cardinal go-getter attitude can help Pisceans make their dreams a reality.

While this sign is devoted to their family and friends, sticking to commitments can be a challenge for many slippery Pisceans. This sign should be wary of over-promising and consequently under-delivering in their eagerness to please and inability to say no. It may seem wrong to a Piscean, but by saying no they might strengthen the bonds that they cherish. Their friends and family are far less likely to get angry if a Piscean says they cannot make a date straight away than if they flake at the last minute. Time management is a skill that might not come naturally to this sign, but it is a tool that they should learn to handle so that they can stay on top of their social calendar. While writing and checking their appointments in a diary or calendar on their phone might not spark the imagination of a Pisces, it will make sure that they don't miss out on spending quality time with their loved ones.

FAMILY AND FRIENDS
· · · · · · · · · · · · · · · · ·

Pisceans can be incredibly creative individuals, and this is often reflected in their enchanting homes. Their walls may be adorned with dreamy watercolour paintings, and visitors might be greeted with aromas of burning incense to welcome them into a spiritual Piscean's home. A home by the sea or lake, where a Piscean can see their element of water regularly, may be where this sign decides to settle. Wherever a parental Pisces lives geographically, this sign usually feels at home. The imaginative Pisces will want to fill their children's life with magic and wonder, perhaps by making sure that Rudolph takes a bite from his carrot or by leaving a coin and a tiny note from the Tooth Fairy. While Pisceans are not generally materialistic themselves, they can be tempted to spoil their children, whose needs they will always put before their own. However, this sign should be careful not to give or do too much for their children. Whether they are a parent, friend, cousin or sibling, a Piscean is ready to bring magic to the lives of others and emotionally support their loved ones.

MONEY AND CAREERS

. . . .

Being a particular star sign will not dictate certain types of
career, but it can help to identify potential areas to thrive in. To
succeed in the workplace, it is important to understand your
strengths and weaknesses to achieve career and financial goals.

While Pisceans usually have fantastic dreams about what
careers they would like to have, they sometimes lack the drive
to make their fantasies a reality. A Piscean can get so lost in
imagining their dream job that they fail to take the necessary
steps to reach their goals. If they consistently underestimate
themselves, it could prove a barrier to making their dreams a
reality. Building their self-confidence might be necessary for
Pisceans to take action. Career paths that spark the imagination
and get the creative juices flowing will appeal to Pisceans.
Whether it's the music of Rihanna or the paintings of Renoir, a
creative Piscean should look to aspirational figures who inspire
them to turn their passion into a career. Another professional
path that Pisces may want to follow is one that allows them
to dedicate their time and energy towards improving the lives
of others. Born in the twelfth house, which signifies service
and sacrifice, Pisceans can be some of the kindest and most
generous souls, so a career as a nurse, aid worker or foster
parent might be best suited to the giving Pisces.

When it comes to a Piscean's finances, money may trickle
through their fingers as quickly as water does. This sign
will not hesitate to buy something that catches their fancy,
which will become an issue if they unintentionally spend

beyond their means. The creative Piscean may have an unsteady income and might struggle to get a grip on their finances and the world of budgets. If the mere thought of a spreadsheet brings a Piscean out in hives, they would do well to find someone else to help with their expenses, particularly if they are self-employed. Earth signs like Taurus, Virgo, and Capricorn usually have a flair for material things, and their practical approach could help a disorganised Pisces handle their money more frugally, aiding them in establishing boundaries and managing their incomings and outgoings. While trusting Pisceans may be tempted to believe in a magical fix to their financial worries, they should be wary: if something sounds too good to be true, it probably is.

While you can't always choose who you work with, it can be advantageous to use your colleagues' star signs to learn about their key characteristics and gain an insight into the best ways of working with them. As a water sign, Pisceans can be swept up in the negative and positive energies of their colleagues, so it's important for this sign to surround themselves with the latter and guard themselves against the former. Pisceans thrive on positive encouragement, so their neighbouring sign Aquarius might be the optimistic and creative influence that helps a Piscean to reach their career dreams.

HEALTH AND WELLBEING

. . . .

Pisceans are the ultimate escapism artists, often living in their own fantasy and choosing to ignore any painful issues in their real lives. However, even with lucky Jupiter co-ruling this sign, their problems won't magically fix themselves. If a Piscean feels themselves drifting into escapism by bingeing on films or playing video games at all hours, they may need to make a conscious effort to come back to reality. While this sign may be tempted to blame others when feeling upset, they might actually be avoiding responsibility for their own mistakes. Pisceans feel things deeply and often internalise their distress. As a sensitive water sign, learning to let go of any emotional pain from the past and focusing on the positives of the present will do wonders for their wellbeing. Practising mindfulness through meditation is a good way for a spiritual Piscean to ease their anxieties and return to a state of calm.

Self-love is important for every sign, but Pisceans can easily forget to nurture themselves while they are busy looking after everyone else. Taking time to indulge their creative side is essential to a Piscean's happiness, but this is something they sometimes sacrifice for the sake of others. If a Piscean has artistic talent, be it with words, art, music or food, they should indulge in their creativity and enjoy the healing magic that is created by doing so. Taking time for themselves may mean that they have less time for others, which can leave them feeling selfish. However, taking even an hour to enjoy a bath, read a book or hone a chosen skill is vital for this sign's health and wellbeing. Once a depleted Piscean has been able to recharge their batteries, they will almost certainly find that they are able to give much more of themselves to the world.

HEALTH AND WELLBEING

Physical activity is a key way for everyone to stay fit, no matter their star sign, but Pisceans are often more interested in stretching their imaginations than their bodies. If Pisces wants to get into a good exercise routine, they should try to find a sport or physical activity that they enjoy while being creative. As a water sign, Pisces could quite literally be in their element while swimming, surfing or ice skating. If water or an ice rink aren't readily accessible to this sign, they might instead dance their way to fitness in a Zumba class or at their favourite music club. Pisceans will no doubt appreciate the creativity of music and dance, while improved health will be a happy bonus for them. While it might be tempting for a Pisces to put on their best heels before hitting the dance floor, wearing comfier footwear could save them some plasters and keep their associated body parts happy and healthy.

Pisces

·················

DAILY FORECASTS
for 2022

OCTOBER
. . . .

Saturday 1st

Although you may want to reach out and broaden your
horizons, your thoughts are likely to be too muddled to do
so today. This might also cause you to doubt your ability to
achieve a dream. If communication with a loved one is tense,
you will have the opportunity to put that right soon.

Sunday 2nd

Mercury turns direct today, but clarity may still evade you.
Take a rest day and enjoy some pampering or connect with old
friends who you trust. Small steps are necessary now, so don't
put in too much effort or drain your resources all at once.

Monday 3rd

Try to begin the working week with a smile on your face and
hope in your heart, especially if you want to shake off the
weekend blues. Get networking: your connections will give you
something to think about which may become useful in time.

Tuesday 4th

Going inside yourself and pulling out old dreams should
give you both a fresh perspective and the space to make your
current dreams happen. You may be torn between joining a
good cause and deepening a bond with a partner. Either way,
there's an opportunity for something to grow and expand today.

Wednesday 5th

You may be faced with a challenge that is also a restriction. Discussing things with your family might show you a way around the problem or help you to make a breakthrough. Talking things through in your mind might overload you with options, so find someone to brainstorm with.

Thursday 6th

The moon is in your sign, and should make for a dreamy day where you feel idealistic and happy. You will be more adaptable now, so anything you are faced with should be easily managed. Go with the flow and enjoy the freedom of movement you have today. It suits you well as a Pisces.

Friday 7th

Relationships should be your main focus now. You may notice subtle changes that make big differences and help your friendships and romantic connections to develop. Conversations may be tricky, but you are likely to achieve the desired result in the end. Your chances of transforming old into new increase when your communication is clear and precise.

Saturday 8th

You are perfectly aligned with your true north today. A weekend activity might lift your spirits, but may mean that you are too busy to spend time with your partner. You should try to involve them to show them their worth.

. . . .

Sunday 9th

There's full moon today, and this should reveal what you value most and inspire you with more ideas than you can cope with. Pluto turns direct, so change is both inevitable and welcome. Take care of yourself and your important relationships, perhaps by organising a Sunday treat.

Monday 10th

If you show a readiness to start the week with a bang, others are likely to notice. You should be more refreshed and feel prepared to tackle anything now. Consider having a conversation you've been putting off. After kickstarting the week, try to settle down peacefully.

Tuesday 11th

Discussions are likely to deepen now, so you may notice that you are more able to talk about difficult issues. Perhaps you want to know more about a partner, especially if you see them as a part of your future. This is a good time to approach the deeper mysteries that fascinate you.

Wednesday 12th

You're likely to feel an urge to break free from the norm today. If there are some restrictions in place, you may have to toe the line before doing your own thing. There will be time at the end of the day to dream, plan and rearrange your reality.

Thursday 13th

Family will be a source of entertainment for you today, although you may find yourself in a leadership role you didn't want. Draw on your research and critical thinking skills, especially if there are many interesting things to learn.

Friday 14th

This is the perfect day to use your mental faculties to bring about more harmony, depth and responsibility. Be on the lookout for a solution to help you manage your time better. Family, relationships and alone time will all benefit you today.

Saturday 15th

Your energy is likely to be focused on family matters and romantic pursuits over the weekend. For example, you could be involved in a family gathering that gives you an outlet for your creativity. This time should be used to protect and cherish those you love most.

Sunday 16th

Try not to jump in at the deep end or talk about subjects others may find awkward today. You have the opportunity to revisit the past and look to the future, so try to blend both nicely. Financial matters might arise, especially concerning investments, shared accounts and legacies, and these might be tricky to discuss.

. . . .

Monday 17th

A rebellious streak runs through your day, so you may consider putting your foot down and insisting that things are done your way. Alternatively, control issues and power struggles could cause you to retreat and defend the things and people you care about. Maintain an unbiased frame of mind where possible.

Tuesday 18th

Remember that duty sometimes needs to come first. If you're being selfish today and ignoring your chores, you may find yourself in a situation you will regret later on.

Wednesday 19th

Use your thinking time to find some much-needed clarity today. Love relationships are highlighted now, especially if both parties have the same agenda, so try to find a partner in crime who is truly on your side. Take your time as you conquer the world together.

Thursday 20th

You are a warrior of the heart today, so what you do is likely to be noted and commended. Put your best foot forward and show the world that you're a compassionate, empathic soul. Try to come across well to everyone.

Friday 21st

This is a pleasant day, so you may be thinking about holidays or long-distance travel and connections. Planning a vacation for the future is usually an enjoyable activity. Look at your past experiences and consider revisiting them, or think about plans for new and exotic adventures further afield.

Saturday 22nd

A partner may need a bit of coaxing to come on board with a plan of yours, even if you sincerely want them to share something you enjoy. Think about involving your wider friendship and interest groups. An earthy, practical activity such as a walk outdoors may be what is needed today.

Sunday 23rd

Are you ready to expand your horizons and deepen a love relationship even further? It may be that you have fallen in love with a new philosophy and are spending a lot more time thinking about it. Saturn turns direct, lifting some pressure from your self-reflection and inner work.

Monday 24th

Your mind and emotions are likely to blend today, and this might help you to discover what makes you and a partner tick. There's an ease to today that can bring harmony and balance to even the most precarious of relationships, especially if you learned more about boundaries from Saturn this year.

Tuesday 25th

Today's new moon and solar eclipse should bring opportunities galore, and this might include the green light you've been waiting for regarding longer holidays or connecting with a new cultural experience. If your heart is calling out for intense experiences that broaden the mind, now is the time to listen.

Wednesday 26th

Reflecting on the past may cause you some tension today. Try not to dwell on what you once valued, as doing so is likely to make you feel miserable. This urge will soon pass, so try not to get stuck in negative thought patterns.

Thursday 27th

A lot of things should be opening up for you now, especially if you have the right amount of energy needed to split time between family and love relationships. If you need to relieve some pressure, try combining these areas of your life. Be aware that you might need to step into the unknown at work.

Friday 28th

Your ruler Jupiter returns to your sign today, which means that now is the time to think about the leaders and teachers who have inspired you in the past. Alternatively, you may find that it's you who has been an inspiration to others recently. Give gratitude to those who have helped form your life.

Saturday 29th

Be careful how you manage your time today, as it's possible that you will tire easily and need more rest. If family matters are draining, try to limit the amount of time you spend on them. Consider making plans for a night out with friends this evening.

Sunday 30th

You may enjoy a seductive time in the early hours of the morning. Mars turns retrograde in your family area today, so collaborative efforts are likely to be futile for now. Energy can be harder to find at these times, especially if things are tense.

Monday 31st

If there's something or someone that isn't good for you, now is a good time to detach yourself. This could be a habit, relationship or situation. Consider retreating and having some quality time to yourself for a while. There may be things surfacing that are difficult to process. Take your time.

NOVEMBER

. . . .

Tuesday 1st

You may feel unable to proceed in one specific direction today, especially if you experience communication difficulties. This phase is likely to pass quickly, so don't wear yourself out trying to get results. Instead, use this time to evaluate lessons learned this year.

Wednesday 2nd

It's possible that you're thinking about relationships from the past or considering how you can better look after yourself. Long-distance connections may offer you something that appeals to a romantic and seductive sense of adventure.

Thursday 3rd

The planetary energy suggests that you will feel fluid, dreamy and mysterious today. You're likely to experience some deep and intense emotions, so follow where they lead. A new spiritual path or self-care practise might be the perfect thing to help you grow and develop. Yoga and meditation are perfect activities for you today.

Friday 4th

If something has stirred deep inside you, look to your inner compass, which should show that you are right on target. Even if you're not full of energy, you might still feel inspired and determined to make the right sort of change in your life. It's time to conquer the next challenge.

Saturday 5th

If the little rebel in you chooses to do exactly what they want, you may find that conversations are narcissistic and get you into situations that threaten to disempower you. Be careful today. Keep yourself in check.

Sunday 6th

You might experience frequent blasts from the past, especially in conversations about or with a person you haven't connected with for a long time. Be wary of secrecy and ulterior motives. Keep your wits about you.

Monday 7th

You may be faced with another of Saturn's little tests today, so ensure that your personal boundaries are strong and healthy. If someone is trying to barge their way into your life without an invitation, avoid a misunderstanding by making your communications to them clear and precise.

Tuesday 8th

A full moon and lunar eclipse occur, and this may bring a close to a recent difficult episode. Try to be fully aware of everything going on today, as it's possible that you will uncover a secret or hear some gossip. Listen well.

Wednesday 9th

The energy is building, so prepare for a potentially volatile outburst. This may be about you or someone else with whom you have been in contact a lot recently. Try to step away from other people's dramas where possible.

Thursday 10th

If you have trouble with your responsibilities today, you might need an ally who can keep you strong and secure. If you're afraid that you might be swept away by the emotional current, try to keep one foot on the ground. Take off your rose-tinted glasses and see a situation for what it really is.

Friday 11th

You're likely to feel drained today, especially if you've lost faith in some friends or family members. It may help to be alone, but you must make sure you're not wallowing in self-pity. Use the time constructively, perhaps by creating art.

Saturday 12th

Romance is often a welcome distraction, and there's enough watery energy around for you to feel perfectly at home, especially if a lover protects you. This is a perfect day for all forms of self-expression, so you may also be in the mood for music, poetry or art. Stay in a safety bubble and create something beautiful.

Sunday 13th

You should notice the benefit of expressing your emotions in this moment. Small changes, surprises and breakthroughs can make dreams come true, so manipulate your own reality and realign with your true north. As a Pisces, you'll probably enjoy swimming in today's ocean. Where will you drift off to?

Monday 14th

If you're floating on this helpful tide, who would you like for company? A teacher or guide may make themselves available today. Use this time to merge with fellow travellers and connect with yourself. Be aware that you may be on show this afternoon, and behave accordingly.

Tuesday 15th

You might have a feeling that something is being taken from you. This isn't quite what's happening, so stay calm. In actuality, you are being asked to make a final effort to go after your desires, so think about planning that holiday or making a romantic move. A phone call may put you on edge this evening.

Wednesday 16th

Do only what is necessary today, especially if you feel your energy slipping away or your focus being shifted elsewhere. This is a result of two planets shifting signs together, and is something you're most likely to notice in the workplace. Keep aware of the things you think you should know.

Thursday 17th

Partner time can help to soothe your mind, especially if you're in a muddle right now. If you feel too emotional to think rationally, those closest to you should know how to sift through the facts and be able to check every detail. The workplace will occupy your thoughts now, so be prepared.

Friday 18th

You should experience a shift from intense inward focus to one that is expansive, dynamic and outgoing, and this could cause some confusion. You may feel irritated with family members today, especially if you're not in the frame of mind to give them the attention that they need. Be patient with them.

Saturday 19th

Today will be exhausting, especially if you have no time to yourself. If you can't keep a lid on your feelings, you might get caught in a row within the family. By evening your mood should lift, enabling you to broaden your thinking.

Sunday 20th

Step up and complete your responsibilities today, as doing so will help keep your mind off any troublesome overthinking. A sense of equilibrium should return, and this will help you to enjoy the remainder of the weekend. It's okay to say no to anything that tips the balance.

Monday 21st

Your busy mind may return to foreign lands and other cultures today. Watching documentaries or doing a little research should satisfy that urge to explore. It's possible that you're about to start working towards a new opportunity that has the potential to raise your status. Go with the flow.

Tuesday 22nd

You may drift back into whimsical thinking today. If deep and intense feelings surface, try to find time to process them alone. The Sun moves into your career area, which means that there might be something bright and optimistic waiting for you just over the horizon.

Wednesday 23rd

If your innermost thoughts are keeping you awake, listen to them. You may experience triggers that ask you to find your edge. In order to make a dream happen, you sometimes need to meet it halfway, so start the ball rolling from your end.

Thursday 24th

There is a huge green light in your career area today. A new moon and your ruler Jupiter, which turns direct, are exactly what you need now. Keep an eye out for a huge career or travel opportunity. If it's right for you, grab it with both hands and don't let it go until you've made the most of it.

Friday 25th

Show others that you are worthy of what is to come. If you're doubting yourself and wondering if you deserve to be rewarded, talk to someone who has more experience and listen to their advice. If you wish to climb the corporate ladder, realise that you already have your foot on the first step.

Saturday 26th

It's a good day to rest and recharge. Pause and reflect on the year and congratulate yourself on your successes. As you look back at past efforts, realise how they have benefited you and smile. Think about the future and visualise yourself there.

Sunday 27th

If you need to tweak something or make changes in your wider circle, you can do so today. You're likely to have luck on your side and vision in your heart. Friends and interest groups are a good source of collective wisdom. Share from your side too, and you will see how enthusiasm can be infectious.

Monday 28th

Try not to start the week on a downer. You need to know that you have what it takes, even if you feel blocked in some way. If this is your own doing, find something that boosts your confidence and lifts your self-esteem. Seek inner strength.

Tuesday 29th

Search your psyche for the resources you need to believe in yourself. Think about times in the past when you doubted your ability but still managed to succeed. An elder or boss might be able to offer you more support. Important conversations are best left until you have more information.

Wednesday 30th

The moon drops into your sign today and helps you to relax.
You may notice that you don't have to put in extra effort
to be noticed, and that others are already aware of your
worth. You could be the ideal person for a certain job, so stop
listening to your inner critic and step into your power.

DECEMBER

. . . .

Thursday 1st

Conflict between different types of energy is likely today, particularly in the workplace. You may need to be extra sensitive, especially if you are caught between two parties that are dear to you. Holding onto your inner compass may save the day, so stay true to your own values.

Friday 2nd

Your sense of justice and equality is likely to be strong today, and respect and responsibility will be vital to overcome any issues. Try not to get too fired up before you know all the facts. You don't get what you desire by rushing into the unknown, so take the time to prepare.

Saturday 3rd

Today should feel much more balanced, allowing you to be more empathetic towards those in trouble. Doing so will be good for you and will bring you a sense of inner peace. You may need to lead the way, but tread slowly and gently.

Sunday 4th

Neptune turns direct today, so you should have greater clarity about your spiritual path and personal ethics. However, be aware that something may knock you from your place of peace. Make this a day of short visits and try to catch up with those who matter to you.

Monday 5th

You might receive a stroke of luck today, and this could propel you forward on your path. The conversations you have will be a key factor, so listen carefully and with an open mind. If you feel an emotional pull, be ready to break free of restrictions.

Tuesday 6th

You may have problems with authority figures or elders in the family today. If you try to keep the peace, you can prevent these problems from becoming a big deal. Keep a tight hold on your dreams and passions and be ready to make a last-minute push to impress the boss.

Wednesday 7th

If today seems too quiet, you may feel suspicious. However, there is no need to fret: this is simply a day where nothing much happens. A midweek family gathering could be the ideal place to be childlike and unfiltered, and this may be exactly the remedy you need. Make time to enjoy a laugh with those closest to you.

Thursday 8th

It's a good time to complete a collaborative project in your family area. The full moon spotlights your communication, but Mars is close, and may induce tension. As always, you can use your gentle persuasiveness to restore harmony quickly. Celebrate any successes and ignore petty squabbles.

Friday 9th

There might be tricky energy surrounding your family today, and this could cause someone to change their mind after an agreement. You may simply have to retreat and let it all die down. Stay safe and protected while keeping out of dramas that don't involve you.

Saturday 10th

Your friendship groups will be a welcome distraction now. If party season has already begun, you may be filling in your planner. Something unexpected that comes in the form of a conversation or message might cheer you up today. Responding with affection and curiosity will likely enhance your day greatly.

Sunday 11th

If you're in need of some fun and laughter, use the remainder of the weekend to think big and let everyone know about your vision. You may feel a little vulnerable doing so, but if you stay true to your soul and speak up, people will want to join in with your enthusiasm.

Monday 12th

You're likely to begin the week feeling more outgoing and optimistic. If you have a passion for life today, spread this feeling around. A challenge may present itself this evening, such as a choice between reconnecting with old friends or making new ones. Consider your options carefully.

Tuesday 13th

If something is blocking your way today, it's likely to be temporary, so don't worry too much. You may be struggling with an issue from the past or words that have opened an old wound. Let everything wash over you and realise that this is part of the healing process.

Wednesday 14th

Seek the affection of a partner who can always talk you out of a low mood, especially if you are doubting yourself and believe that your dreams are unattainable. Turn to your wider friendship groups for support and plan a midweek get-together.

Thursday 15th

Have you noticed that you are far more grounded today? As a water sign, this is unusual, so make the most of it. You may be able to slow down and choose a single path from many. Remember that pausing isn't the same as stopping.

Friday 16th

It may feel like you have lost sight of your inner compass again, and this could be because you are being overwhelmed by the need to consider things such as friendships, interest groups and social media contacts. You might reach out, or find that someone reaches out to you. A good cause may need your input, but make sure you have a moment to breathe.

Saturday 17th

If socialising isn't on your agenda today, that's okay; you're allowed to switch off and have alone time. You might notice an underlying feeling that keeps you from connecting with friends. What is brewing for you? Is it just a tremor, or is it a potentially dangerous eruption?

Sunday 18th

Stay out of manipulative situations today. Your heart and head are unlikely to be in sync, so you may make poor decisions. Act in a mature manner and be respectful at all times. By evening you may find that this tension has passed, allowing you to think more clearly.

Monday 19th

Even if you are harbouring feelings of mistrust, your friendship groups can provide a source of lively communication. You may be thinking of travelling with a close friend or partner and planning a new adventure that combines work and pleasure.

Tuesday 20th

Your ruler Jupiter leaves your sign today, so you should now feel its jubilant, lucky influence in your life. This is exciting news and may enable you to make big plans for the coming year. Watch out for people who push too far or demand too much from you.

Wednesday 21st

Today is the winter solstice. The shortest day of the year is the perfect opportunity to host a gathering of friends and reflect on the events of 2022. You may get lucky at work and catch the eye of someone influential, or a colleague might suggest a celebration in readiness for the festive season.

Thursday 22nd

Your energy might be low today, but you can still enjoy a few surprises with friends. If you receive an invitation from someone you haven't seen for some time, it may be difficult to commit to a meeting, but a phone call or message may be enough to facilitate an enjoyable reconnection.

Friday 23rd

Get ready to party. A new moon is the start of the festivities and heralds a shift in your friendships, especially if you're looking at joining new groups next year. Volunteering or taking a leadership role within an interest group could be your new calling and might result in a rise in status.

Saturday 24th

This is a great day for socialising, communicating and generally having a good time, so celebrate in style this evening by letting luxury dining and good conversation kick off a very special gathering. You can expect to feel more at peace and in love with everyone around you today.

Sunday 25th

You may feel the broader effects of this day, especially if your sensitive soul is on red alert. The empathy you have for your closest friends and family will be limitless, while your excellent self-control should make you the perfect host. You may be the star of the show, but try to give equal attention to all.

Monday 26th

It's possible that you feel a little deflated today, and this is only natural. If everyone is tired, conversations will be far quieter. You may notice that you need to refill your own cup, particularly if you have given too much from it recently. Do your duties as you need to, then relax.

Tuesday 27th

The moon returns to your sign and should lift your spirits. The fun and games may still be going on, and you will have the right amount of energy to join in. If you want to relieve any pressure you feel about choosing who to spend time with, simply go with the flow.

Wednesday 28th

You may once again feel more tired than usual. Go easy on yourself today and allow for a few treats. If your friends and your inner compass combine, you will feel certain you are on the right path. You may also feel supported and encouraged by your colleagues and interest groups. Take a leap of faith.

Thursday 29th

Mercury turns retrograde today, so you should back up your devices and be careful with all travel arrangements. People might say more than they mean right now and could also be prone to gossip or expressing love more readily than they intend. Keep yourself safe and slow down.

Friday 30th

It's possible that you will have trouble staying still today, while also finding it difficult to make any kind of progress. Family matters might feel strained or exhausted, so keep a low profile and stay away from troublesome dynamics. Recharge ready to party tomorrow night. Don't push any complicated issues.

Saturday 31st

You're likely to be in the mood to celebrate, but first you may need to be the mediator in a situation between two people. This could be a challenging evening, but with a lot of self-control, you can come out of it as the winner and be the one who restores harmony.

Pisces

....

DAILY FORECASTS
for 2023

JANUARY

. . . .

Sunday 1st

Set your resolutions for the year and either write them down
or say them out loud. It's a powerful day to make plans and
voice your wishes for the year ahead. If there's someone you've
been wanting to speak to, make it happen. You may have to let
go of a friendship if things are too complicated.

Monday 2nd

Remembering someone from your past is a way of keeping
them with you. Take the time to write a letter or pick up the
phone and share your memories with someone close. Use the
long weekend to reach out to other people and make deep and
meaningful connections.

Tuesday 3rd

Personal matters may dominate, especially if you find you
are drawn back into the past. Keep strong emotions out of
the equation where possible. Instead, stick to the facts and
be honest, especially when dealing with a challenging or
unsettling situation.

Wednesday 4th

If you're harbouring strong feelings, do you want to try to
rekindle affections, or is it time to move on? Love has a private
or hidden theme now, and this could lead to the reignition of
an old love affair, a blast from the past or a reconnection with a
childhood sweetheart.

Thursday 5th

If a good friend needs you now, you may have to drop everything and step in to help. If so, the experience might be powerful for both of you. Focus on teamwork and group collaborations in the workplace, as this is where success lies.

Friday 6th

You may be looking to resolve a personal situation or close a door on the past during this full moon period. Tie up any loose ends in your life so that you're ready to move ahead and get on with things. Being with the ones you care about is both fulfilling and nurturing, so prioritise love and happiness.

Saturday 7th

It's the midpoint of the Mercury retrograde phase, and this is a time of illumination and insight. For you, this may be linked to your friendships and your role within a group, club or society. You might decide that it's time to explain your recent actions or decisions to someone close.

Sunday 8th

The beginning of the year could be momentous if you reconnect with a friend you've lost touch with or you spend time with a family member in a way that's deep and meaningful. The theme is a return to the past. A new friendship may begin in a surprising way.

Monday 9th

You're likely to be a caring soul, so you should try to find the time to check up on someone in your life. It's a good day for heart-felt connections. It is important, however, to keep on top of your work and health goals too.

Tuesday 10th

Whether you had a late night or you sleep in this morning, it might not be the most productive start to your day, especially if you feel exceptionally tired or under the weather. It's a good idea to focus on tasks that are manageable and easy.

Wednesday 11th

This might be a tense time for family relations, especially if you're caught in the middle of an argument between your partner and one of their family members. Alternatively, the problem may be that you and someone close don't see eye-to-eye. Talk to a good friend and ask for their advice.

Thursday 12th

If you don't like the direction a home or family matter is going in, think carefully about how you want to handle this. Today's stars hint at a turning point and a chance to clear the air, although it's unlikely to be a harmonious shift.

Friday 13th

You're likely to be happiest when your relationships flow smoothly, so any impulsive behaviour on your part may be a reaction to what's going on in your personal life. A caring friend will be a big help. Keep talking about a home or family issue.

Saturday 14th

Life will be easier if you can deal with your close relationships in a way that's objective and rational rather than emotional. Aim to do things that help you feel more balanced inside, such as spending time with the person who knows how to calm you and soothe your soul.

Sunday 15th

Don't worry if you have a tricky start to the day, as you should be able to get back on track quickly. Deal with your finances promptly today to ensure you feel more secure as you start to make some plans for the coming year. It's good to have something to look forward to.

Monday 16th

Turn your attention to your vocation and life goals today. If you're not in your work stride yet, this is a good week to focus on your next steps. If someone keeps bothering you by text or online, it might be best to switch them off. It's probably not worth the aggravation.

Tuesday 17th

If you're typical of your star sign, you'll find that it's important to pay attention to the emotional rhythm of your day. Learn to work with your energy levels rather than against them. If there are times in the day when you're less productive or more tired, tweak your schedule accordingly.

Wednesday 18th

Mercury, the planet of communication, turns direct today in your friendship and group zone, and this means that it's a good time to reach out to someone who's been quiet. The theme of endings is important now, so you may decide that it's time for you to leave a group or to move on in some way.

Thursday 19th

This isn't a week where you can drift through life, as much as you might like to. There's a get-real theme to the week's astrology that encourages you to make a new commitment towards your future and your long-term goals.

Friday 20th

If some time out is called for or you want to relax, the stars are in agreement. At the very least, try to organise some personal time and prioritise self-care. It's a good weekend to work on any personal issues, so listen to your inner voice and trust your intuition.

Saturday 21st

A fresh start beckons during today's new moon, and this may coincide with an inner experience. This is about you, your outlook on life and your way of thinking. Try to wrap things up from last year or complete a project you started some time ago.

Sunday 22nd

It's important that you deal with life head-on today, so try not to avoid any sensitive issues. It's a good idea to switch off the news and social media and enjoy an information detox. Tap back into your emotional state and let it guide you.

Monday 23rd

Be there for your friends, especially if there's someone who's going through a tough time. Your compassionate and caring nature is being called forth, so try to be of service to others.

Tuesday 24th

The moon in Pisces encourages you to seek comfort and nurture in your personal life. Let go of a home or family issue and try not to get involved if things are argumentative or noisy. A gift that's linked to your past may appear.

Wednesday 25th

If you're typical of your star sign, you're a sensitive soul, so it might be best to put clear boundaries in place concerning other people. If you find that you're constantly picking up on the emotions of others, learn how to shake off those energies so that they don't weigh you down.

Thursday 26th

You're wise to put your interests first right now. Sometimes you have to be more self-centred to feel secure in a specific situation. It's a good day to trust your luck, while your belief and hope may prove equally powerful.

Friday 27th

Love planet Venus enters Pisces today, and this is a sensitive, compassionate and caring influence. It's a good time to find your muse, go on a date or fall in love. Do more of what's important to you and try to move away from any challenges or sadness in your life.

Saturday 28th

Try to stay close to home and catch up with your neighbours or enjoy a community event. You may be taking lots of short trips to the shops or meeting up with relatives. A busy vibe will suit you best today, so extend the web of communication.

Sunday 29th

It's a great day to use the internet to find out information or share news. Whether your tweet goes viral or you discover the perfect online course, there's plenty of excitement and innovative ideas available.

Monday 30th

If an important matter has been going on for a while, it's a good day to be proactive and look for solutions. There may be a way to go before the project's finished, but you have an opportunity to make some big steps forward today.

Tuesday 31st

Continue what you started yesterday and consider getting a member of your family to help out. You might also find that you're trying to get to grips with a family matter that's dominated for too long. There may be a turning point in the middle of March, so plan accordingly.

FEBRUARY
. . . .

Wednesday 1st
It may be easy to lose track and get diverted from what you're meant to be doing today. If there's a task you want to complete, try to find somewhere quiet where you can concentrate. Too much noise at home or in the workplace will prevent you from being productive.

Thursday 2nd
If you have a generous spirit, it may kick in first thing today. However, it's important to be clear about your motivations, as it sometimes seems easier to give someone what they want, even if it doesn't serve them in the long run. Love is in the ascendancy, so a lunchtime rendezvous might be thrilling.

Friday 3rd
It might be a good idea to say no to a friend's invitation, especially if you don't have the energy to deal with their problems today. Instead, try to do more of what you love, whether it's a hobby or a creative activity.

Saturday 4th
If you've been feeling out of sorts recently, it's a good weekend to focus on your health and wellbeing. Make an effort to exercise, eat well and recharge your batteries. Too much digital stimulation can damage your sleep patterns, so consider spending some time in nature instead.

Sunday 5th

Today's full moon highlights your work and health, so it's a good time to get the balance of life right. Take time out if you need to, or put in some extra hours to complete an important job. Prioritise organisation and do whatever's necessary to get on top of things.

Monday 6th

Love and friendship are likely to be linked today, whether you're pleased with a friend's news or you enjoy a good connection with someone you've known for a long time. It's an ideal day to strengthen the bonds between you and someone close, so try to practise love and compassion.

Tuesday 7th

It might be better to avoid getting caught up in another person's family problems today. This is even more important if you need to pay close attention to what's happening at home. Helping other people can make you feel better, but it's important to concentrate on your own issues too.

Wednesday 8th

What you may be lacking in confidence, you may gain in acclaim or popularity. It's a good time to boost your image, so think about planning a beauty session or makeover. A compliment has the power to make you feel good on the inside as well. Remember that love and spontaneity go hand in hand.

Thursday 9th

It's a good time to move away from personal matters and seek fulfilment elsewhere. When it comes to love and relationships, try to iron out any issues between you to ensure you're both on the same page.

Friday 10th

There's a theme of endings today, of letting something or someone go. You may have to say no today, especially if your awareness of a situation is particularly relevant. Any decision is likely to be final, so try to stand by what you say.

Saturday 11th

There might be times this weekend when you sense that you're out on your own walking an independent path. If you're moving on from something, you may need to reschedule a friendship or group engagement.

Sunday 12th

Steer away from petty arguments and look to the bigger picture of life instead. It's a good time to think about your travel or study plans as well as your next steps. Seek inspiration and broaden your mind. Try to move away from the everyday.

Monday 13th

You might find it challenging if you're supposed to be at work and getting on with things today. Recent events may have left you feeling unfulfilled or unsure of what to do next. Try to prioritise your own needs and be wary of rushing into anything new, especially if you're lacking confidence.

Tuesday 14th

Today's stars suggest that you're back in the driving seat and ready to take on the world. Focus on your career and look at ways of improving your situation. It promises to be a romantic Valentine's Day, so make the most of it.

Wednesday 15th

Today's stars are blissful and divine. There may be an opportunity to lose yourself in love, so long as you remember that business and pleasure don't mix. Be clear about where your priorities lie. You may need to think about choosing between love and your ambitions.

Thursday 16th

There may be a lot to consider today, especially if a personal issue is weighing you down. If someone else has control over you or you're feeling the strain of recent events, take things slowly. Your confidence should get a welcome boost once the Sun enters Pisces in a couple of days.

Friday 17th

If you're a typical Pisces, you're likely to have many different friends in your life. Right now, it may be best to be around those who know how to lift your spirits and offer a shoulder to lean on. Today, give less and be open to receiving more.

. . . .

Saturday 18th

The Sun's move into Pisces is a positive shift, so you should feel a surge of vitality and energy. If you've been struggling with responsibilities or you're dealing with an ending in your life, refocus your attention on your health and wellbeing. It's your turn to shine.

Sunday 19th

Consider spending the day with the person who makes you feel good about yourself. Start to think about your next steps as you reorient your goals and aims. It helps to look forward to making hopes and wishes a reality.

Monday 20th

Use the power of today's new moon to write down your intentions. The Pisces energy is gorgeous for magical thinking, so allow yourself to be inspired and uplifted. Step out of your comfort zone, treat yourself and do whatever's needed to boost your confidence.

Tuesday 21st

Don't start the day with an argument if you can help it, even if this means steering clear of anyone in a bad mood. Your thinking may be erratic now, so it will help to stay away from the news and harmful gossip. This evening, lose yourself in a good book, a feel-good movie or a candlelit bath.

Wednesday 22nd

There might be good news regarding money matters today, potentially in the form of a gift or bonus. It may be a good time to treat yourself, perhaps by spending time with a book or film this evening. Think about getting back in touch with a family member that you haven't seen in a while.

Thursday 23rd

If you need to talk finances with someone in your family, try to have a productive conversation. This should help you understand what's been going on over the last few months. Try to manifest more of what you want in your life.

Friday 24th

Consider asking other people to help you out today. Not only will you get more done at home or in the workplace, you'll also have more fun. There's an easy flow in your stars, so consider staying close to home if you need a source of stability. Nurture new friendships and strengthen your support system.

Saturday 25th

It might be a challenge to get off the phone today, especially as your communications look lively. You may catch up with a family member or lose track of time chatting to the neighbours. It's a good day to stimulate your mind by doing puzzles or listening to an educational podcast.

Sunday 26th

Your community and network can be a strong source of support and information in your life. Reach out to other people and nurture your local connections too. When you make an effort to engage with other people, it can benefit your life in many exciting ways.

Monday 27th

If you've been avoiding a member of your family, return to the matter at hand and try to work out a mutually amicable solution. A turning point may come later next month, but good cheer and goodwill should go a long way towards improving relations for now.

Tuesday 28th

If there's something in your life that you're worried about, don't feel that you have to sort everything on your own. Even if you're the one who usually comes up with good ideas, it's likely that other people can help.

MARCH
....

Wednesday 1st

If you were up late last night, you might not get a lot done today. The moon highlights play rather than work, so you're wise to do more of what you love. Be around people who lift your spirits, such as family members.

Thursday 2nd

Your stars look wonderful and abundant, so consider doing something nice for yourself or the ones you love. If there's something that's gone unsaid for far too long, you may find that it can't remain hidden any longer. Think about speaking up and voicing your concerns.

Friday 3rd

If someone close to you is behaving oddly, you might need to find time to talk things through with them. If they're experiencing intense emotions, they will probably appreciate a chance to let off steam and voice what's bothering them. At the very least, you should ensure that they know that you're there for them.

Saturday 4th

If you've got a great idea, this is a good weekend to get busy and make it happen. If it's something that would help other people in some way, you're probably on the right track.

Sunday 5th

It's a good day to prioritise your health and fitness, especially if you can find someone to help you to do so. Team up with a buddy or ask someone in your family to walk or run with you. It's a great day for a family activity, so gather those closest to you and make the most of it.

Monday 6th

You may find that you have no choice but to take life seriously right now. If you're a typical Pisces, you'll be happy living in a fantasy world, but that doesn't mean you can ignore what's going on in reality. Deciding when to say no is often more important than you realise.

Tuesday 7th

Today's stars suggest that you might step into a new position of authority or run into a limitation that slows you down. Either way, it's time to make an important decision. The light of the full moon is encouraging you to close a door on your past.

Wednesday 8th

You might be lost in a haze of romance or feel sentimental about someone who's no longer with you. Tune in to your emotions and follow your intuition, as doing so will help you to know yourself better.

Thursday 9th

It's a good idea to look for help right now. Consult with other people, especially if you're dealing with an important issue. If it's been an emotional few days, try to remain objective about anything that's come to light and aim to do what's best for everyone concerned.

Friday 10th

You're right to be upset if someone isn't being fair or honest with you at the moment. If this impacts your family, even more reason to get fired up. Try to channel your anger constructively. Try not to give in to any unreasonable demands, however intense or emotional someone feels.

Saturday 11th

Whether you're writing your CV or talking about yourself, now's a good time to get your voice heard. Find people that want to listen to you and use technology to amplify what you have to say. There's a theme of unity and support at home.

Sunday 12th

It's a good day to revive your dreams for the future. If you're looking for a way out of a challenging situation, think about lining up an escape route. Take yourself off somewhere new, as doing so will provide the breath of fresh air you're seeking.

Monday 13th

You may have to let someone know that you're not the right person for the job today. If you're feeling the weight of responsibility, consider your limits and manage expectations.

Tuesday 14th

You may be disappointed or disillusioned with a member of your family today, or you might find that you have to let go of a long-held dream concerning where you want to live. Try to let things be rather than blaming someone else.

Wednesday 15th

Keep your dreams alive by diving deep into activities that stir your imagination. Try to seek inspiration through reading, learning and connecting with other people.

Thursday 16th

If you feel lost or confused today, it's a good idea to keep a tight hold on your emotions. Find new ways to stay connected and keep the lines of communication open. Ask for help and support when you need it and offer the same in return. Let go of any anger or past hurts.

Friday 17th

You may be called forth to help other people communicate today, so find your voice. Prepare yourself to talk to a group of people or to step into a leadership role. Find the best way to express yourself so that everyone understands you.

Saturday 18th

Take some time out and create some space for yourself this weekend. If a lot's been happening and you're feeling unsettled, engage with activities that restore a sense of balance. Use this time to switch off and detox.

Sunday 19th

Consider adopting a leisurely pace today so that you can recharge your batteries. Be there for others but ask for support and help as well. Talk things through and ensure that other people listen to what you want. Find a way to lessen the burden you're carrying.

Monday 20th

Your money zone is in the cosmic spotlight, so energy and clarity are required. A fresh burst of enthusiasm and some proactive initiatives should help. The equinox heralds a new season and may offer a chance for a fresh start, and this will lift your spirits and boost your confidence.

Tuesday 21st

Today's new moon highlights money matters, so it's a good time to set your intentions for the future. State your desires out loud, write things down and get clear about money and how it relates to your self-value.

Wednesday 22nd

Opportunity and good fortune lie wherever you find lucky Jupiter in your horoscope, and right now Jupiter is boosting your money zone. It's a good time to get in touch with your entrepreneurial nature by coming up with some new ideas.

Thursday 23rd

It's an important time for friendship and group connections. Things may have already changed in this area of your life, especially if you're in the process of letting go of something. You might need to drop out of a group or move away from a friend who doesn't understand you.

Friday 24th

There's a whiff of romance in the air today. Seeking love could provide the excitement you crave and take your mind off other areas of your life. If you're in a relationship, think about ways to keep things fresh.

Saturday 25th

Today's stars may prove momentous, especially if they coincide with the end of a home or family issue that's been dragging on for way too long. There might also be good news about romance and passion, so be ready.

Sunday 26th

If you're stepping into a new role within your family, you might be worried about what any new developments will mean for everyone. Use this time to talk things through. It's a bittersweet day with the potential for excitement and regret.

Monday 27th

Keep looking to the future and aim to close a door to the past firmly behind you. Other people may look to you for the nod of approval or to be the responsible one in the family. This might come as a surprise, but it's time to start valuing yourself fully. Don't let a confidence issue hold you back.

Tuesday 28th

If you want to have an important conversation, this is a good time to do so. If you approach things with the right attitude, you're more likely to get the answer you're looking for. A new romance might take off quickly, so be prepared.

Wednesday 29th

If things have been happening too fast recently, slow things down and bring it back to basics. As one of the water star signs, you're likely to respond to life emotionally. It's a perfect day to spend quality time with the ones you love.

Thursday 30th

The theme of romance remains under passionate stars, so it's a great time to seize the day and declare your true affections. Someone close may be upset about what's happening, but you also need to consider your needs and the life you want to live.

. . . .

Friday 31st

As a Pisces, you're likely to have a sensitive nature. If other people have recently let you down or you feel bewildered by everything, even more reason to be clear about your purpose and motivation. Try to find nourishment and fulfilment in your life, and move forward with clarity.

APRIL
. . . .

Saturday 1st
You may have to swap your schedule around today, especially if there's an unexpected opportunity that's too good to miss. You may have to disappoint someone by cancelling a social get-together, but sometimes it's worth putting more energy into your other activities.

Sunday 2nd
If you're up and active early this morning, you're in tune with your stars. It might be a tricky day, especially if you're not happy in love, and your attention is likely to turn to your relationships later on. If you're feeling gloomy or tired, it could impact your interactions with other people, so make an effort to be upbeat.

Monday 3rd
It's a good day to ditch a negative mindset or bad attitude. You might need someone to talk to, especially if a relationship is tense. You could talk to a sibling, a neighbour or someone in your local community. Ensure you have a supportive network of people around you.

Tuesday 4th
It will be difficult to make sense of a close relationship if you're feeling confused or unsure of your emotions. It's a good day to talk things through with people close to you. Make time to reconnect with friends and the people who matter most.

Wednesday 5th

Be ready to have an important or official conversation today. This may take the form of help or advice, either for you or someone else. Being positive will go a long way. It's an excellent day to sit a test or exam.

Thursday 6th

Full moons are a great time to trust your intuition and find solutions to problems. It's good to be there for others but you also have to take care of yourself, so consider your self-worth and how you value yourself. Listen out for insights.

Friday 7th

You should find that you're full of creative ideas about how to spend the Easter weekend. You might be inspired by art, beauty, music or prose, leading to strong feelings of compassion and care for the world and the people in it. Think about spending time with your favourite family member today.

Saturday 8th

You may change your plans this weekend and stay closer to home rather than travelling further afield. If this means you can have a heart-to-heart with someone close, then it's a good idea. Make time for the person who approaches you later on.

Sunday 9th

If you're feeling dissatisfied with where you're heading, try not to let this spoil your Easter weekend. You may originally have planned to focus on your career and vocation today, but that's not where the emphasis lies. If you're pulled between different priorities, put people first.

Monday 10th

This is a good time to focus on your future goals, so fire some arrows into the sky and see where they land. Get excited and inspired by the people around you. There's some good fortune on the horizon.

Tuesday 11th

This could prove to be one of the luckiest days of the year, and this is great news if you're about to make a big step or decision. What happens today might signify a new chapter in your relationship with a member of your family.

Wednesday 12th

Tensions could flare first thing, so be careful you don't overreact to a friend's drama, even if there's a lot of anger and hurt flying around. Look for support closer to home and turn to the person who gives the best advice.

Thursday 13th

The past will impact the present in some way today. Be careful that you don't turn your anger on yourself and instead learn to release any difficult emotions constructively. It might not be the best idea to spend too much time reminiscing or mulling things over.

Friday 14th

There may be a disappointment today, especially if you feel disheartened about an important situation. Try not to overreact to what occurs, unless you feel that you need to put firm boundaries in place. Take some time out this evening.

Saturday 15th

You may want to address recent events today, but don't put yourself out to do so. Instead, consider waiting for another person to come to you, as they might provide a rapid solution. Be aware that your confidence may currently be tied up with your values and your ability to look after the ones you love.

Sunday 16th

You may be getting used to a new responsibility in your life. Whether other people are turning to you to make key decisions or you're taking life more seriously, it's a role that's likely to suit you. Knowing your own mind will have a positive impact on your relationships.

Monday 17th

Turn your attention towards your image, goals and aims. It's all about you today, so put your needs first and let other people see who you are and what you have to offer. If your imagination is a powerhouse of ideas now, use it to the full.

Tuesday 18th

You may be spending time working on your home, especially if you want to make it more beautiful. Wait until after Thursday's eclipse before making any big moves, then plan your next steps.

Wednesday 19th

Your money values will be important now. You might have an opportunity to put a lesson you've learned into practise, as this is a good moment to make a conscious decision. If in doubt, ask an expert for advice.

Thursday 20th

Today's eclipse lights up your money zone and is the start of a two-year period that could change your earning potential. Remember, there is often a correlation between confidence and financial success.

Friday 21st

Mercury turns retrograde, and this might cause a few hiccups or false starts. You may hear some news today that's disappointing or discover that you have to play a waiting game for the next few weeks. Try to learn from what you've discovered and be brave as you move forward.

Saturday 22nd

You will have the opportunity to help a family member or someone you live with by giving advice today. If you're aware that you're often in tune with other people, trust your instincts and make someone feel better. Tough love may also be required.

Sunday 23rd

If you fancy yourself as an interior designer, today's stars are perfect to turn your hand to decorating or styling your home. It's a good day to invite everyone around to your house for a meal or some time together.

Monday 24th

You might have a job on your hands if you're trying to cheer up someone who has received disappointing news. A little treat or some kindness will go a long way. It's also a good time to retake a test or exam.

Tuesday 25th

It's an ideal day to think about some new arrangements with someone close to you. If you're not ready for the next big step, it's important to be clear about this. Communication is the key to a healthy relationship.

Wednesday 26th

You should discover a new level of self-discipline, and this will come in useful if you're learning an instrument or language or you want to get fit. If you're typical of your star sign, you're likely to be creative and artistic. Hone your skills.

Thursday 27th

You might experience frustration first thing today, especially if you're not getting the answers you need. Be aware that this is a time where misunderstandings and delays could occur. Double-check all forms of correspondence and don't leave anything to chance. Be vigilant at work and at home.

Friday 28th

It's not the best day for a meeting or presentation, so you might need to think about rescheduling an important interview or conversation. A member of your family should know exactly how to cheer you up this evening.

Saturday 29th

It could turn out to be an exciting day for someone in your life; they might win a contest or sporting event or pass an important test. You might be up for some fun and games yourself, and this is also a great evening for a first date.

Sunday 30th

If you're with a long-term partner or you're married, it's always good to try and put some work into your relationship. Make sure you don't negate your own happiness. When you reconnect on an emotional level, you can see the way forward.

MAY

. . . .

Monday 1st

The spotlight is on relationships right now, but it's also a day
for some deep thinking. You may feel more introspective than
usual and need some time alone. It's important to listen to
your inner voice, so don't ignore any uncomfortable emotions
that you experience.

Tuesday 2nd

The stars instruct you to aim for more balance in your life
today. If you're in a quandary about a close relationship, look
at your situation objectively. If an issue has gone on for a long
time, consider your next steps carefully.

Wednesday 3rd

On the surface, things might look composed and you may
seem to have everything together, convincing everyone that
you're doing a good job of keeping things ticking over. In
reality, however, you might be paddling away like mad below
the surface. Swallow your pride and ask for help.

Thursday 4th

You may experience a romantic and sentimental pull towards
your past. It's a wistful time full of yearning and longing. You
might feel disheartened if you're unable to focus on your own
life, but you may need to prioritise family. Let the moon's light
guide you to the right course of action.

Friday 5th

Today's lunar eclipse has the potential to be deep and passionate for you. It's a time for adventure, new experiences and a desire for something more from life. See what occurs today that calls you forward and find where you can make changes.

Saturday 6th

Your soul may be restless, especially if you're yearning for something more. This feeling may have started a couple of years ago, around the second half of 2021. It's not the best time to make a big decision about travel or study.

Sunday 7th

Love planet Venus makes a move, so love and romance are highlighted now. This means that it could prove to be a dreamy few weeks for your love life and close connections. Focus on the positives in your life.

Monday 8th

It's always good to have something to look forward to, so consider exploring travel options or a new course of study. Nothing is set in stone right now, so you may find that you change your mind more than once. View this as the research stage that comes before a decision.

Tuesday 9th

Your life might be super busy and dramatic today, especially if an unexpected encounter leads you in a new direction. Seek expert help or ask for ideas to resolve an ongoing issue. Your local community might be a good place to find answers.

Wednesday 10th

It's a good day for spontaneous interactions. Consider sending an email or text, contacting someone out of the blue and exploring new ideas. You're wise to act fast in all forms of communication, especially first thing. Think twice before revealing all to an old friend.

Thursday 11th

Take some time out if you can today, especially if recent events have left you feeling particularly wired. It might be best to avoid a conversation that you suspect is going to challenge you. If you can, wait until after the weekend before revealing your plans. Get an early night if you're tired.

Friday 12th

This might be a tricky day for your close connections, and things could turn out to be super lively. Someone may try to persuade you to help out in your community or look to offer advice. If this isn't welcome, don't feel that you have to say yes.

Saturday 13th

Your dreams may be especially revealing this weekend, so listen carefully to them. A love relationship could move on to a firmer footing if you become more sure of your feelings. Family matters are also likely to be important.

Sunday 14th

If you feel more confident and sure of yourself today, it means that you're ready to have an important conversation, so consider reaching out. You may have a significant interaction with a sibling, relative or neighbour, perhaps about a new study course.

Monday 15th

Mercury turns direct today, so you should listen out for important news and information. It's a great day to launch a website and get up to date with new technologies. It's important to be proactive and get things moving where necessary.

Tuesday 16th

Opportunity planet Jupiter lights up your communication zone, so you're unlikely to be short of ideas from today. Your ability to learn and share what you know is also highlighted. Think about making new friends, getting involved in your community and using social media to expand your contacts.

Wednesday 17th

This is a great time for collaboration. Reach out to other people and find your voice to ask for what you want and need. Look out for new people who come into your life. Implement your best ideas to build the best future.

Thursday 18th

Words have extra power today, so you might find that you want to speak up for others or expose an injustice or wrong-doing. You may also be at loggerheads with a person who disagrees with you. Try to keep a level head.

Friday 19th

Today's new moon is ideal for making connections. It's a perfect day to consider launching a community project or starting a blog or podcast. Spend time this weekend working out what you want to say and communicate with others.

Saturday 20th

Work and health matters will become important from this weekend onward, so you might find that you're busier than you have been in the past. If you're looking for work, it's a good time to apply for a job; if you want to boost your fitness levels, think about a new regime or schedule.

Sunday 21st

You may need to work overtime if you have a tight deadline to meet this weekend. It's also possible that there's a contract or some other work coming to an end. If this is true for you, release any frustrations first, then turn to someone in your family for help and guidance.

Monday 22nd

You might have to work out a new schedule today, especially if you're starting a new job from home. Work and time management are key areas of your life right now, so be proactive and work as part of a team, either in the workplace or within your family.

Tuesday 23rd

It's a day of excitement and enthusiasm, but there's the possibility that things could go completely over the top. If you've started a lively fitness regime or you're trying to do too much at work and at home, take care. A lunchtime rendezvous may provide welcome relief.

Wednesday 24th

Things could reach a crisis point today, especially if you've taken on more than you can handle. Try not to get pulled into an argument at work and be extra wary of office politics. If a colleague's being overly difficult to be around, it might be wise to look for support elsewhere.

Thursday 25th

You may be keen to complain about someone else's behaviour or to gossip about them behind their back, but a more constructive response would be to focus your time and energy on getting the job done. If you have no choice but to work together, try to find ways to adapt.

Friday 26th

The workplace may continue to be a challenge for now, so if you have the chance to change things around to work from home or otherwise alter your usual routine, this might be a good idea. If you want a quick boost, turn to someone close for some positive affirmation.

Saturday 27th

When it comes to a close relationship, it's important to remember why you fell in love in the first place. If there are currently challenges in a long-term relationship or marriage, don't allow what's not working out to dominate. Make an effort to get on with one another.

Sunday 28th

You may need to think about laying down the law today and putting some clear boundaries in place. Try to create healthy relationships at home and keep the lines of communication wide open. When you're honest, everyone benefits.

Monday 29th

It may be a challenge to keep those all-important boundaries in place this morning. If your emotional nature takes over, you might find that you give in to other people too easily. Get back on track by agreeing on compromises that work for everyone.

Tuesday 30th

Any partnership fares best when there's an equal amount of give and take. If the balance of a relationship is currently out, it might be time to confront the issues head-on. Appeal to a person's sense of fairness to get the changes you want.

Wednesday 31st

You may be teaching someone about the nature of sharing today, especially if you need to divide an important responsibility with a partner or someone close. You might not always agree with one another, but it's probably worth trying to sort things out between you.

JUNE
. . . .

Thursday 1st
If you get to work and immediately end up in an argument, try
to tackle the issue head-on. You may have to find somewhere
quieter to work, or you might need to let a boss know what's
going on. Don't let any fears stop you from taking charge.

Friday 2nd
If a partner keeps coming up with the same problem, try an
alternative approach. It's a similar solution wherever in your
life you're having the same conversation over and over. When
it comes to a love relationship, romance wins every time.

Saturday 3rd
If you find that your home and family life is dominating right
now, it might be difficult to pursue your career goals. If you
know the work/life balance is out, play around with new ideas
during this full moon weekend.

Sunday 4th
If things come to a head today, listen to what life is telling you
and decide what steps you can take to move things in the right
direction. You'll feel happier if you can create more time to
focus on your goals and aims. This evening is the ideal time to
initiate an important conversation.

Monday 5th

If you're back at work, now's the time to gather support and get the right people on your side. Your job happiness is often directly linked to your relationship with your colleagues. If there's a personnel change, your working life might suddenly feel a whole lot easier.

Tuesday 6th

It's a good day to focus on your hopes and wishes, so think about lining up some firm plans for the future. There's strength in numbers, so gather the right people around you. This evening, take the time to socialise with your friends.

Wednesday 7th

Be wary of intense emotions today. Even if you're normally kindness personified, you might feel angry now, perhaps because someone in your life has behaved out of order recently. Don't harbour resentments and try not to create any extra drama in your life.

Thursday 8th

It's a good time to take a step back and engage less actively with life, especially if you don't have a strong grip on your emotions or you feel tired or stressed. Turn to someone in your family for some extra help or support. Approach any problems with an analytical eye.

Friday 9th

If someone's been there for you consistently over the last couple of months, reach out to them. If this person has continually offered help or guidance, what they have to say now might be exactly what you need to hear.

Saturday 10th

It's important to try to put your needs first today, so let your family know that this is what you're doing. The moon in Pisces encourages you to be compassionate and kind to yourself. Seek stability in your life and calm your emotional compass, especially if it's been swinging wildly in recent days.

Sunday 11th

When you stop and you're quiet, you can pay attention to your inner voice. Trust your insight and dig deep to get a better handle on an important issue. It might only take one conversation to help you resolve a painful personal issue. Be with your family and loved ones today.

Monday 12th

Attack the working week with gusto. It's a good day to get fired up and motivated, especially if you're busy at work. The more confident you are about your self-worth, the easier you make things for yourself.

Tuesday 13th

Work alongside other people to boost your confidence. Your self-worth is an important factor in your life, and when you let go of negative thoughts, you'll find a fresh reserve of energy. Top up your confidence levels.

Wednesday 14th

Be around the people in your life who make you feel good about yourself. It's a great day for affirmations and positive thinking. When you help people, you often benefit emotionally. It's a good day to join in with a community venture.

Thursday 15th

There are only so many balls you can keep juggling at the same time without dropping them. If you're trying to be everything to everyone, something might have to give. Take off one of your many hats and reduce the time and energy you allocate to others.

Friday 16th

If there's anything you want to change at home or something you need to discuss with the people you love, your cosmic opportunity will arrive this weekend. Today's stars provide you with a chance to heal a rift, perhaps by spending time reminiscing with the people closest to you.

Saturday 17th

Don't rush into anything this weekend, and instead use this time to reassess things. Prevent yourself from heading off down the wrong path by turning your attention inward and slowing down the pace of life.

Sunday 18th

Today's new moon brings a spark to your home and family
life, and might lead you to consider somewhere new to live
or to work out your options around an important deal. It's
an excellent day to prioritise family matters and initiate key
negotiations, as doing so will put your mind at rest.

Monday 19th

You may start the week feeling confused about where you're
heading and why. Try to ride the waves of life and go with the
flow; don't worry too much about the end destination for now.
Instead, focus on the journey, even if you're unsure where
you're going to end up.

Tuesday 20th

You may not always feel that you're someone who's especially
wise, but someone might see you as the person to turn to
now. Trust that you know how to help other people, especially
the ones you love.

Wednesday 21st

Turn your attention towards the aspects of your life you enjoy
the most. Take up a hobby, fall in love and rediscover where
your passion lies. Even if there are serious issues in your life
right now, try to tip the balance towards fun and play.

. . . .

Thursday 22nd

If you want to create better working relationships, now's the time to try. It might help to look at a tense situation from the other person's point of view. When you walk in someone else's shoes, you often develop a deeper understanding not only of who they are but also what they require.

Friday 23rd

Make time for love and relationships today. Get together with the person you care about for a late lunch. You may learn a lot from someone in your life, and it's a good day to show that you're willing to listen. This evening, close the door on the world and feel content.

Saturday 24th

Spend time with the person you love the most this weekend. A relationship prospers when you know that you're bigger and better as a couple. If you require some feel-good vibes or acknowledgement, ask someone you trust for help.

Sunday 25th

Get creative about home and family matters today. If things have gone awry, look for new ways to get back on track. Try not to be disillusioned if your home life isn't ideal. If you want more time to yourself, visit your place of retreat and escape.

Monday 26th

If you're fed up with the antics of a work colleague or someone you see every day, it might be time to press the eject button. Remember that you don't have to put up with their nonsense; take yourself out of the equation. Keep calm and avoid taking unnecessary risks.

Tuesday 27th

If you were up late last night talking to someone close, you may not feel as tired as you expected; you might even be feeling energised because of what you discussed. It's always good to know that the ones you love are on track and doing well. Your mood is likely to impact your work today.

Wednesday 28th

It might be best to avoid a friend's drama, even if they are having an emotional time. You may do yourself more of a favour by concentrating on your life and plans. Gather some much-needed strength and think about future opportunities.

Thursday 29th

Manage your schedule well over the next couple of days. If you want more time to devote to a hobby, start by getting organised. If you're typical of your star sign, you may need to work on effective time-management techniques.

Friday 30th

Be clear with the people and things in your life that keep you grounded. When you commit to the ones you love, this acts as an anchor for you. Decide what you're going to give your focus to, whether it's your masterpiece or some creative artwork.

JULY

· · · · · · · · · · · · · · · · · · ·

Saturday 1st

The weekend has some definite feel-good vibes, so try to make the most of them, especially if you're attending a party or celebration. If you believe you'll have a good time, it's more likely that you will.

Sunday 2nd

You may need to think about detaching yourself from a working relationship that's grown complicated. Notice if you've been trying to impress someone or been desperate to make friends. Take an objective look at the situation and act accordingly.

Monday 3rd

When you teach and inspire the people around you, it reminds you about the important things in life. Enjoy today's sociable and celebratory full moon by focusing on simple pleasures, such as kindness and enjoyment.

Tuesday 4th

You may need to deal with a friendship that's become intense. If someone's behaviour is too much for you, take a step back. It's important to remember that powerful emotions can get you into trouble. Make some time for yourself this evening.

Wednesday 5th

If you've come unstuck recently, you might be wary of revealing your thoughts or emotions to another person. As a Pisces, you're likely to have a generous nature, but you may sometimes need to rein it in. Think about creating more privacy in your life and choose your confidantes carefully.

Thursday 6th

It's a good day to be an observer, so watch what other people are up to. Work is the obvious place to do this, especially if there's a lot's going on. If you're not in the workplace, think about your everyday environment. You might be surprised by what you learn.

Friday 7th

You might find that you're experiencing loneliness in your life or realise that you're craving more solitude than usual. Accept what's changing and shifting within you, and ensure that, when you do want to chat, there are people that you can talk to.

Saturday 8th

It's a dreamy kind of day, so you may struggle to get a lot done. Give your imagination full rein, go with the flow and choose to do whatever you please. If you're a creative type, it's a great weekend to be an artistic genius.

Sunday 9th

Pay attention to what's going on around you, as doing so may lead you to uncover an important message. If you've been learning lessons, they might lead you to discover where fulfilment lies. Encourage your mind to dream deeply.

Monday 10th

You may be up against a tough competitor over the next few weeks or find that there's someone in your life who doesn't cooperate. One way or another, you're likely to be at a period in your life where you're questioning what other people mean to you and how best to deal with them.

Tuesday 11th

There's a sociable side to your work and connections today. If you can get together with people you work with or see daily, this is a good time to do so, especially if you need to ask for support. It's an excellent day to apply for a job.

Wednesday 12th

You might have to change your plans without much notice, especially if you find that you're on the move more than usual. Technology may be both a blessing and a curse today; for example, you could find out the information you require, but it might also take you ages to sort out a problem.

Thursday 13th

If you're trying to juggle too many commitments today, something may have to give. It's a good day to multi-task, but don't expect everyone you encounter to be easy to deal with. If someone close lets you down, turn to a family member for help.

Friday 14th

Try to look on the bright side of life today. Enjoy the sunshine and be around people who lift your spirits. Your close connections should be especially fulfilling now, and this includes friends, family and anyone who is important to you.

Saturday 15th

Working out how to deal with close relationships can take up a lot of your time and energy. The truth is that sometimes there are no right answers. So long as you're doing your best, that's enough. Getting on the right side of your work colleagues is always a wise move.

Sunday 16th

Embrace more of what you love today, especially relatives and the loving connections in your life. If you're in a happy family, spend some quality time together. If you're on your own, line up a social event to lift your spirits.

Monday 17th

Today's new moon falls in your play zone, so it's a good day to focus on the things in life you enjoy. Try to enjoy the sociable aspect of your job and find a way to use your skills and talents outside of work.

Tuesday 18th

There should be a shift from play to work by the end of this week. If you love what you do, work might feel like fun, and enjoying yourself can sometimes be your vocation in life. Spend some time today ensuring that your daily routine works for you on an inner and outer level.

Wednesday 19th

If there's anything you're worried about at your place of work, consider lining up a meeting to get your questions answered. You may want some time out over the next few weeks, and you might also hear a rumour that someone's leaving work.

Thursday 20th

Consider how you can remain open and ready to help others, even in the face of a challenge or opposition. If there's a toxic individual in your life, it might be time to shut the door and move on. Someone may have to prove their commitment to let you know whether they're in or out.

Friday 21st

There's a chance that your stars will bring more passion your way today. However, if you're in a relationship, things could become challenging, and this might also apply to a personal or professional partnership. It's always a good idea to look for some good advice.

Saturday 22nd

Don't let someone close pull the wool over your eyes today. If you're typical of your star sign, you trust easily, sometimes too much so. If someone is making your life difficult, you may need to think about putting a stop to things immediately.

Sunday 23rd

Over the next few weeks, it's important to define what work means to you and to consider how you want to spend your life on a daily basis. Be more aware of the connection between mind, body and spirit, as doing so will bring some clarity to your daily activities.

Monday 24th

There might be a surprise at work first thing today, and your situation may change as a result of the behaviour or actions of other people. Be flexible, but know that everything may not work out as planned.

Tuesday 25th

If you're worried about the financial implications of recent events, talk things through with a someone you trust. If you want to book a holiday or study break, other people may be able to help you.

Wednesday 26th

If your plans have changed, you might be thinking about booking a holiday later this year. Don't lose faith in life, and instead try to be proactive in pursuit of your goals. Get the right people on your side. Don't give up.

Thursday 27th

Time spent with someone you work with or a person you see most days will be especially welcome today. Talk and catch up this afternoon; you may also find that you're able to help each other with an issue or dilemma. The more sociable you are with work colleagues, the happier the working environment will be.

Friday 28th

Continue to work towards your career or vocational goals and don't be dissuaded if someone tries to put you off. It can be wearing if there's someone in your life who continually says no. A late-night conversation may help to bring understanding and insight to a key relationship.

Saturday 29th

It's a good day to focus on where you're heading in life. If you're fired up, join forces with another person, as you'll get more done together. You might find a new gym buddy today.

Sunday 30th

There are some days when what you want most is to catch up with an old friend that you haven't seen in a while, so take the time to enjoy a lengthy conversation with the person who knows you best. Being around someone wise will help you a lot.

Monday 31st

The emphasis on building good connections in your life
remains strong today, so turn to your old friends for advice.
Alternatively, you might choose to reach out and try to make
new friends online.

AUGUST

. . . .

Tuesday 1st

Full moons often bring matters to a head, and for a Pisces like you, this is about getting your life in order. This might mean sorting out your workspace, prioritising your wellbeing, or something else entirely. Take a holistic approach to your life and focus on your mind, body and spirit.

Wednesday 2nd

You may have to focus on lots of different people in your life at the moment, even if you're aware that there's a divide between some of them; for example, one person might be adventurous, enthusiastic and encouraging, while another person may be negative and likely to bring you down.

Thursday 3rd

It's not always easy to speak up, especially if what you have to say is difficult. You might need to challenge someone close about their behaviour, especially if their actions impact you. Try to stand your ground, even if you need to be cruel to be kind.

Friday 4th

Your role in other people's lives remains significant. You may not want to dampen someone else's enthusiasm, but you might need to offer some criticism or feedback. Try to do so in a way that makes it easy for the other person to hear.

Saturday 5th

The fire signs - Aries, Leo and Sagittarius - are often motivated and energetic. Get excited about any fire sign activity that you pick up on today. If you have a situation that's urgent, now's the time to leap in.

Sunday 6th

The right connections will be a big help for you today, especially if other people's ideas seem spot on. It's worth checking out your finances, as you may be throwing money away on something you no longer use.

Monday 7th

Be wary of a person who promises more than they can deliver. At the same time, be open to someone who wants to give you support at work. It's a fine line to walk, but you may receive a welcome boost if you judge the situation correctly.

Tuesday 8th

Use your local connections and networks. If you have an entrepreneurial spirit, an online group should fire up your enthusiasm. It might be worth thinking about a course, as you could learn a lot in a short amount of time.

Wednesday 9th

Someone might let you down through no fault of their own today. Be aware that something related to work or fitness may be cancelled. Be understanding, especially if the person concerned is having a difficult time.

Thursday 10th

Other people remain important to you, perhaps even more so than usual. You might have to rely on others in a new capacity, or you may find that someone takes on a significant role in your life. Repay them with kindness.

Friday 11th

You may find yourself caught in the middle of a family situation. Perhaps you're trying to juggle conflicting personalities in your home or current living situation. It may not be easy to find a solution, but it's worth persisting.

Saturday 12th

This is a great weekend for love and romance. If you're looking for a new relationship, maximise your chances of success by getting serious about your intentions and letting people know. There may be a connection with someone you met previously.

Sunday 13th

Today's stars suggest that you will reconnect with someone close on a deep level. Even when life gets busy, make time for others and prioritise meaningful connections. Try to create healthy, supportive relationships in your life.

Monday 14th

It's a good week to be more ambitious about your work and fitness, so be ready to act fast and make things happen. Whether you want to get fit, leap into a new work role or boost your mental wellbeing, you should find that you have added drive and determination now.

Tuesday 15th

Keep your eye on the prize today. Get the right people on your side and take advantage of expert advice. Team up with others to move your life forward in a positive way. It's not a week to do things by yourself, so aim to work alongside other people.

Wednesday 16th

Today's new moon means that it's an excellent day to set your intentions and start a new routine that benefits your everyday work and wellbeing. You might find the perfect job through an online advertisement, so be alert.

Thursday 17th

You may need to consider being cautious and defensive in your close relationships today. If there's one person you're continually struggling with, try to be around them less. You might have to dig deep, especially if you're feeling sad or lonely.

Friday 18th

You may gain some insight about what's going on in a close relationship today. If you want to talk, consider arranging to meet after work this evening. If it's an issue related to your job, ask the other person if they're willing to meet up outside of work hours.

Saturday 19th

It's a good day to turn your attention to love and relationships and to reconnect with someone close, especially if you need to sort out any issues between you. It may take a while for love to develop fully, so be attentive and keep talking about the things that matter to you.

Sunday 20th

Think of today's stars as an opportunity to recalibrate your inner scales and find some much-needed calm. Be around people in your life who help you feel balanced. Ensure it's a day packed full of healthy food, enjoyable exercise and laughter.

Monday 21st

Start the week as you mean to go on by prioritising your wellbeing in all areas of your life. The more responsibility you take for your happiness, the easier life becomes. Rely on yourself more now and over the next few weeks.

Tuesday 22nd

Any ongoing relationship challenges will be highlighted today, especially if you recognise that there's an imbalance in one particular area. It's also important ensure that you're not being a victim or a martyr. Some things may have to change, so try to work them out between you.

Wednesday 23rd

Mercury turns retrograde today, highlighting misunderstandings and untruths, and causing things to become complicated. It's a period when you will need to wait and be patient. It's not the best time to make a major decision about an important issue.

Thursday 24th

Turn your attention to your work, especially if it provides a welcome escape. If someone's gone quiet on you, leave them alone for now. If you're repeatedly analysing a relationship, work on your internal state. If someone's reappeared in your life, take your time as you get to know them again.

Friday 25th

This should be a time of healing and transformation when it comes to love, so consider what this means for you. Someone who's back in your life may have reawakened your passion, and this might cause conflicting feelings. Whatever your situation, turn inward for answers.

Saturday 26th

If you're a typical Pisces, you may sometimes spend too much time in a fantasy world rather than reality. If so, take care that you don't let someone pull the wool over your eyes. Be honest about what's happening in a close relationship and seek a friend's advice if necessary.

. . . .

Sunday 27th

Recent events may have made you aware that some things
need to change within a relationship or business partnership.
You might want to consider some new boundaries or rules
as you think about your next steps together. Work things out
between you.

Monday 28th

You may have been up late last night, especially if there's a lot
to think about. Talking things through can help, so long as you
avoid going round in circles. It may help to take a step back
and prioritise some quiet time. Don't make any rash decisions.

Tuesday 29th

You may find that you change your mind and want to take
back something you said recently. However, it's important to
be wary of being overly impulsive and to consider your inner
motivations. A powerful full moon is on the way, and this
should shed more light on your current situation.

Wednesday 30th

You may be tired today, especially if your sleep is disturbed
during this emotional full moon phase. You might find
yourself feeling lonely, and there may be a tough decision to
make. You might not be a naturally sensible person, but now is
the time to look after yourself.

Thursday 31st

Today's full moon might coincide with the pinnacle of a
love relationship, causing you to fall in love all over again.
Alternatively, now may be the time to search for answers.
Either way, you're likely to learn a lot about yourself, especially
when you see yourself mirrored in the lives of others.

SEPTEMBER

· · · · · · · · · · · · · · · · · · ·

Friday 1st

Try to align yourself with people you can trust and rely on this weekend, such as a long-standing personal or professional partner. Be on the lookout for the nudges of the universe.

Saturday 2nd

Trust your intuition, especially if you're taking on a project that leaves you feeling out of your depth. Money matters may be important right now, so move swiftly and decisively. The more information you have, the better.

Sunday 3rd

You might need to find a loophole or a way out of a situation. It's a good day to focus on money matters, so look at your outgoings and pinpoint where you can make savings. If a good friend needs your help, offer emotional support.

Monday 4th

Two planets switch direction today, so you need to focus on what's working well for you and look out for the person who can help with what isn't working. The planetary switch may also spell good news for a fellow employee or someone close. It's a good day to think about what you want to stay and what you want rid of in your life. Readjust your needs.

Tuesday 5th

You're likely to be buzzing with gossip, especially if you're talking about someone's love life or have discovered some juicy information. If you want to know more about what's going on, talk to a neighbour or relative.

Wednesday 6th

Today is a good day for a heart-to-heart with someone important in your life. A surprising turn of events might change a situation in a good way, so watch out for a magical moment when you could hear the news you've been waiting for.

Thursday 7th

Your home and family matters are under the cosmic spotlight right now. Rather than worry too much about things, you're wise to focus on your current commitments. Shoot off some emails, get on the phone and sort things out.

Friday 8th

This weekend is a promising time to reassess your personal relationships. Decide where your heart lies and consider putting new boundaries in place. Be around the people who build you up rather than those that bring you down.

Saturday 9th

Joyful relationships make the world go round. The best thing you can do today is be with the ones you love, so line up some fun times. Consider revisiting one of your favourite childhood activities, as doing so may prove to be a cathartic experience.

Sunday 10th

It may be better to avoid a friend who's having a crisis, so put yourself first by instead trying to boost your own feel-good vibes. Even if you know you need to get organised later on, you should be able to spend most of the day indulging in whatever activity brings you happiness.

Monday 11th

Good relations can boost your life in more ways than one; for example, you might make friends with an influential colleague or meet someone who has a great piece of advice. Reach out to other people today and create a good support network around you.

Tuesday 12th

Concentration isn't a typical trait of your star sign, so you may have to adopt some tricks to ensure you stay focused on the job at hand. Technology problems might be disruptive today. Pace yourself and try not to work beyond your capabilities.

Wednesday 13th

This week's new moon promises a fresh start, so it's a good idea to look closely at your personal relationships now. If there's someone you want to talk to, line up an intimate conversation this evening. If something's bothering you, now might be the time to voice your concerns.

Thursday 14th

Decide where your alliances lie and which conversations you feel need to happen. When it comes to both your personal and professional relationships, this is not the time to procrastinate. Line up an important meeting or interview and speak from the heart. Say what you have to say.

Friday 15th

The new moon takes place today and may indicate a new phase in your relationships. Think about joining a group, being committed and working hard to keep hold of the people who matter to you. Someone you encounter today might be the catalyst for a new adventure.

Saturday 16th

Communication planet Mercury is back up to speed, so you should have the information you require to make an important decision and get things moving. In love and business, don't settle for less than you deserve. To keep a relationship vibrant, it's important to embrace new experiences together.

Sunday 17th

You may have to think about cutting someone off if they've caused you too much pain. Sometimes you need to get rid of the deadwood in your life, and doing so will allow new moon energy to flood in.

Monday 18th

Turn your focus away from relationships and out into the world. You might need something to look forward to that broadens your horizons and expands your mind. Make either travel or study your first port of call and have a look at both of these areas in detail.

Tuesday 19th

You may not always perceive yourself clearly, especially if you've put someone in your life on a pedestal. Avoid detrimental comparisons to others and remember that criticism and nagging often have little to do with love or respect. Don't waste your kindness on someone who doesn't deserve it.

Wednesday 20th

It might help to adopt a broader perspective on life today. If the opportunity arises, say yes to going somewhere different. Notice who or what is blocking you or holding you back. If it's fear, think about how best to boost your confidence.

Thursday 21st

Your partner may not be the best person to turn to for advice now, especially if they are finding it hard to help you make a clear decision. Instead, place your trust in an expert or adviser and share your questions and worries with them. Alternatively, look to the friend who knows you best.

Friday 22nd

Now is a good time to consider your image and how you come across to other people. If you sense that your true worth isn't being recognised, take a closer look at what you're able to change. Once you take yourself seriously, other people are more likely to do the same.

Saturday 23rd

There's a feel-good factor to your stars today, so make the most of it. Be around people who boost your confidence and make you feel good about yourself. You might benefit from another person's triumph or celebrate alongside them. The right partnership will boost your energy.

Sunday 24th

Friendships and group endeavours are where the action's at today. Join in with an activity that's specifically designed for your generation. Spending time with people who are experiencing the same things as you can be a revelation.

Monday 25th

You may choose to extend an olive branch today. Alternatively, someone in your life might come to you to ask for forgiveness. If there's a conversation that never materialised over the summer, it's a good day to initiate it. Reconnect with someone close in a way that's deep and meaningful.

Tuesday 26th

You might prefer some quiet time to be alone with your thoughts today. Do some research or prepare for a new project or chapter in your life. Switch off from the digital world and turn off the noise where possible.

Wednesday 27th

The moon is in the safe harbour of Pisces today, so you should focus on your emotional needs, especially if there's something you're lacking. If you want more affection or support and guidance, ask for it. A late-night phone call may prove to be worth staying up for.

Thursday 28th

Focus on the karmic connections between you and your family or someone special in your life. Understand that some things just work without an explanation. Explore more of life's mysteries and be open to weirdness and wonder.

Friday 29th

Today's full moon highlights all forms of money matters. Draw up a spreadsheet and make sure you know what's going in and out of your account. Make sure you're doing what's best for yourself and your family.

Saturday 30th

A third party may have some exciting information for you today. If you receive good news, you will probably want to share it with someone close to you. Use your communication skills to dazzle them, then celebrate together.

OCTOBER

Sunday 1st

If you're ready for a real conversation, this is your opportunity.
It's easier to talk when there are no distractions, so consider
walking with a friend in the countryside. Try to do whatever
anchors or grounds you today. It might be comforting to find
out that another person agrees with you on the big issues.

Monday 2nd

It's not a good idea to let other people get away with things
today, especially if you're not happy with the way things are
being handled in certain areas. If you're pushing a new agenda
through at work, ensure the right people are on your side.

Tuesday 3rd

If you're unsure about someone's suitability for a job or role,
dig a little deeper by following up on a previous conversation
and asking more pertinent questions. If you don't know how to
handle an issue at home, reach out to a good friend.

Wednesday 4th

It's a good day to delve into family finances and think about
your future security. Team up with your partner to tackle a
difficult issue together and work alongside other people to
bring more harmony and stability into your life.

Thursday 5th

Turn your attention to money and finances and open the lines of communication. The more you find out about money matters, the more you are likely to benefit. If you need help, get some expert advice.

Friday 6th

While it can be hard to put in the work to make the people closest to you happy, the benefits you receive in return are often invaluable. It's a good time to discuss an important issue with someone close today.

Saturday 7th

You might get a reality check over the next few weeks, especially if something important falls through, or something you expected to receive fails to materialise. Consider your options and cover all bases.

Sunday 8th

You might encounter a difficult conflict today, but it's better to avoid getting involved if you can. You may discover who your friends are and who's not on your side now. If you've made any enemies in your life, proceed cautiously, as someone may want revenge.

Monday 9th

Love planet Venus moves into your relationship zone today, and this indicates a new phase in your close relationships. If you're looking for love, write down your cosmic wish list. In all areas of your life, the right partner can make a huge difference, so choose wisely.

Tuesday 10th

There's a nod to the past when it comes to love and relationships today. Your first instinct may be to pull back, but sometimes you're better off being with someone who knows you well, especially if you've already put in a lot of work together. Consider your options carefully.

Wednesday 11th

Someone may be playing a power game today, so proceed cautiously. If you've recently split up with a partner or ended a business venture, you might discover which friends are on your side and which aren't. Steer clear of any potentially risky situations where possible.

Thursday 12th

A new phase begins, so you will likely be itching for a change of scenery or feel a yearn to study something new. Think about how you can broaden your horizons over the next few months.

Friday 13th

It's all well and good having dreams and envisioning your future, but it's important to have a long-term plan to turn your dreams into reality. Ask a friend to help you take the first step towards your goal.

Saturday 14th

Today's solar eclipse urges you to look at your money motivations. Do you believe you're good with money, or do you hand these matters over to other people? Does money arouse strong emotions in you, such as guilt, envy, fear? This is the ideal time to delve a little deeper.

Sunday 15th

If you hang out with someone who you think of as being courageous and bold today, they may inspire you to get moving with your plans for the future. Strive to live your best life and use this opportunity to increase your motivation levels.

Monday 16th

If you're a typical Pisces, you're likely to have a wide social network. If you want to get clear about your next steps, now's a good time to turn to your connections for help. Spread your net far and wide and reach out to other people via social media.

Tuesday 17th

It's always a good idea to ask more than one person the same question, as that way you'll get a few different answers. Not all of them will be right, but at least one of them may bear fruit. It's the same as sowing seeds – some will flourish while others fail, so scatter those ideas wildly.

Wednesday 18th

Each of us plays many different roles in our lifetime. You might begin to realise that you've almost outgrown one of those roles and that you're ready for something different. Take a closer look at your long-held dreams and see if there's one that's worth nurturing.

Thursday 19th

It's good to get another pair of ears to listen to your thoughts and ideas. If possible, speak to someone who can be objective about your current situation. You need to consider the implications of what you're planning, and this is where you may require some expert advice.

Friday 20th

If you're discussing an important issue today, consider getting some expert advice. Look to find security in your past, your family and by working together with the people closest to you. It's a good day to work out an agreement that suits everyone.

Saturday 21st

There may be an opportunity to let go of a draining obligation or commitment today. The stars feel intense, so you might need to deal with a situation that's been hidden from you. Avoid power games where possible.

Sunday 22nd

If you're struggling with a difficult situation, a relative or family member might surprise you by offering to help. It's a good time to think about your education, and to offer someone a helping hand.

Monday 23rd

The Sun enters a star sign that works in harmony with your own, so you're likely to feel in your element today. Boost your feel-good vibes and look for ways to expand your horizons, such as travel and education.

Tuesday 24th

This is a positive time to learn a language or sign up for a course of study. If there's something you've been wanting to explore for some time, take that difficult first step today.

Wednesday 25th

Someone who comes into your life now could be the catalyst that makes you want to learn more about something new. Encourage your other half to expand their horizons and think about signing up for an exciting activity together.

Thursday 26th

If you've recently discovered your ambitious streak, now's the time to channel your drive and determination. This will be especially pertinent if you're about to change direction or embark on a new chapter in your life.

Friday 27th

You may be keen to make some extra money today. Whatever your motive, this is an excellent time to focus on finances. You may have to act quickly, so don't procrastinate. Make sure you don't spend what you haven't earned.

Saturday 28th

Eclipses often provide an opportunity to take advantage of a power shift, so be alert, as you may be up against someone with different ideas to you during today's lunar eclipse. It also helps to be patient and understanding when the situation calls for it.

Sunday 29th

This is a good weekend to go on an adventure and look for new experiences. You might have a conversation or read something that stirs your interest, or someone else's intervention may spark a sudden rush of desire on your part.

Monday 30th

There's a lot of astrological movement currently taking place, and this will translate into people moving in and out of your life. Consider opening your doors to a person in need.

Tuesday 31st

Love and new connections are often linked. Now's the time to do something different with a loved one, so think about booking a trip together. Look for a chance at romance.

NOVEMBER
· · · · · · · · · · · · · · · · · ·

Wednesday 1st

It's not the best day to deal with life's practicalities, so you may need to rely on someone else's help. If you're handling something important, double-check the arrangements. This evening, feelings of commitment may kick in.

Thursday 2nd

Consider making plans for a holiday or weekend away. You'll also be excited if you're planning to see someone in the family for the first time in ages. A social get-together might quickly grow in size and be more fun as a result.

Friday 3rd

It's always good to have something planned that you're looking forward to. Try not to read too much into recent events and be aware that, if you expect a lot, you're more likely to be disappointed. Be excited but keep it real.

Saturday 4th

Dig deep into your reserves of strength and willpower today to get everything done. A serious matter may seem tedious, but it's rarely a good idea to ignore important issues. If you feel strongly about a personal goal, now's the time to find the power required to start moving things forward.

Sunday 5th

If your plans change suddenly this weekend, make time to regain your balance. Be on the lookout for some unexpected news, perhaps from abroad or concerning an educational course. Whatever the case, allow your emotions to settle before you decide what to do next.

Monday 6th

If you feel out of sorts first thing, you might end up being late to work or an appointment. Try to shake off any upset and lower your stress levels. When it comes to love and relationships, you may want some reassurance this evening. Have a serious conversation.

Tuesday 7th

You might have placed a lot of importance on an upcoming holiday or trip away, especially if it's a big deal for your relationship. Laughter and good times will be a big help now, so don't miss the chance to hang out and have some fun.

Wednesday 8th

It's important to share your responsibilities with your other half. If one of you is taking on a bigger role, it may not sit easily on the other's shoulders. Find a way to create more balance in your partnerships.

Thursday 9th

There could be a boost to your money situation today, perhaps as the result of a gift or payment that you weren't expecting. If you want to earn more money, use your connections and ask around for ideas. If you're thinking about gaining new qualifications, it's a good time to dive in.

Friday 10th

If you're looking for work or want to boost your prospects, you're in tune with your stars. This is the ideal time to ask around, so send off some applications and find out more. At the same time, work on your confidence levels to prevent a lack of self-esteem from holding you back.

Saturday 11th

You may be required to dig deep now, especially if you run into some disappointment or rejection. Don't be disheartened, but do ask for feedback and think about what you might be doing wrong. Tomorrow is a new day.

Sunday 12th

Think about taking yourself off somewhere new and different today. You may want to find some incredible views to gaze at, whether you're by the sea or you head for the hills. A change of surroundings should help to put recent events into perspective. Reorient your mindset so that you stay positive.

Monday 13th

You're probably going to be keen to say yes to a new adventure during today's new moon. Travel and study may inspire you, even if you're focused on the future. If you attend an online course or you're on a call, be aware that some technical issues may cause a delay.

Tuesday 14th

Try to deal with any fears head-on: you don't want self-doubt to put you off lining up an interview or meeting. Today's a great day to impress other people, so use your communication skills to your advantage.

Wednesday 15th

It's a key day to talk about work and money matters, so get some expert advice. It's also a good time to think about lining up a job interview. Pursue your goals with gusto: aim high in life and up your game. Try to impress the right people.

Thursday 16th

Slow things down and take stock of how far you've come. If life's been busy recently and you've been moving at a fast pace, catch up with the essentials. It's a good idea to hang out with your old friends and spend time with the people you feel most comfortable around.

Friday 17th

Keep hold of your dreams and breathe new life into them. This forward-moving phase of the moon encourages you to set your intentions and, more importantly, see them through. If you need new dreams to inspire you, draw up a vision board or experiment with mind-mapping.

Saturday 18th

When it comes to a travel or study opportunity, this could be the time to pull the trigger, especially if you've done all the research and asked for other people's opinions. Follow your instincts and do what's best for you.

Sunday 19th

You deserve a day to relax and take it easy, so it's a good idea to pause your plans and put any commitments on hold. Spend the day relaxing and doing what you love. Recharge your batteries for the days ahead.

Monday 20th

Tempers may flare first thing, perhaps leading to an argument on your way to work. Try not to get involved in any trouble. You may have to make time for yourself later on, especially if you need to finalise something or you're busy studying.

Tuesday 21st

It's a good day to work on your confidence skills, so consider turning to the person in your life who already believes in you and is great at reminding you of your strengths and talents. Ensure you're well prepared for your next steps.

Wednesday 22nd

The Sun lights up your career and vocation zone from today onward. This is the peak of your horoscope, so it's an ideal time to reorient your compass and think about what's next. Be flexible, consider all your options and talk things through with the people who inspire you the most.

Thursday 23rd

There may be something that you have to let go of if you're going to pursue your chosen goal or the next stage in your career. This could be an outdated perception of yourself or a responsibility that you're ready to pass on. Get serious with yourself and others.

Friday 24th

Tap into your potential as a leader and, if you're ready to do so, take a big leap in life. Focus on where you're heading and take some bold steps. Your stars indicate that you may have to step up your game to compete.

Saturday 25th

When you make bold moves in life, it's inevitable that you'll run into an obstacle or setback. What's important is that you don't let this stop you from being ambitious. Be open and willing to learn from your mistakes and listen to the people in your life who know you best.

Sunday 26th

It might be worth making an early start today, whether you're meeting someone for a run or you're having a leisurely breakfast. Stay close to home, catch up with the neighbours or attend a local community event. Everyday affairs will bring you back down to earth, and this can be a good thing.

Monday 27th

It's a positive week to discuss what comes next and where you're heading. This is the perfect time to line up some long-term goals, especially if this helps you to generate more excitement and enthusiasm. Notice where disillusionment lies, as this could provide the impetus for your next move.

Tuesday 28th

You may require the support of your family and loved ones now, especially if you're setting off on a new adventure or taking a step forward in your career. Try not to feel guilty if you don't have as much time as you would like for the people closest to you. It's a good time to line up some new goals.

Wednesday 29th

Get some support if you need it today. When you have a strong base and a good network around you, taking those next steps becomes so much easier. The people closest to you usually know how best to help.

Thursday 30th

It's a good idea to line up an event that's frivolous and fun today. If you want to accept a spontaneous invitation, cancel whatever's in your diary and say yes. Remind yourself of the things in life that you love and do whatever feels right for you.

DECEMBER

. . . .

Friday 1st

If you're a typical Pisces, people matter to you deeply. Reach out to your friends and make connections that can help you in your career and vocation. It's also important to fulfil your sense of wellbeing, so arrange a night out, let your hair down and have some fun.

Saturday 2nd

You may have to work this weekend, especially if you've picked up a part-time job before Christmas or you're busy in your regular employment. Do your best to find time to reunite with an old friend if they've made the effort to come and visit.

Sunday 3rd

It's worth double-checking your budget before you rush out and start buying Christmas presents. You wouldn't want to be surprised to discover that you have less money than you thought. View any upset as an opportunity to get back on track. Next week is a new beginning.

Monday 4th

Love will have an exotic feel over the next few weeks, so your heart may desire things beyond the obvious or expected. It might help to have something to look forward to, such as an activity that takes you beyond your everyday routine. If you want your life to be extraordinary, expand your world.

Tuesday 5th

Go that extra mile today, especially if you want to reconnect with someone who lives abroad or you're keen to persuade your other half that it's time for a holiday. Someone from your past may get back in touch and reawaken your feelings.

Wednesday 6th

As a Pisces, hopes and dreams are likely to be integral to your life, so fire up your imagination and awaken your creative side. If things are something of a muddle, it might help to surrender to life and trust that it will lead you on the right path.

Thursday 7th

Turn your attention towards work and money matters today. If you're keen to earn more, consider what your next steps might be. If you want more stimulation at work, consider what you need to help you to grow and develop in your career.

Friday 8th

If there's someone in your life you promised to be in touch with, try to reach out today or over the weekend. You might want to write a letter or send a card with photos attached that acts as a reminder of the big events of your year. Clear your diary and get organised.

Saturday 9th

It's a great weekend to visit relatives and catch up with friends you haven't seen for a long time. Consider making the effort to travel to visit them, especially if you feel a change of scenery would do you good. If you're looking for love, you might meet someone at a workshop or educational course.

Sunday 10th

Things may not go according to plan later on today, so leave yourself plenty of time, especially if you're travelling on a long journey or going to the airport. Communication planet Mercury is getting ready to slow down, so it's wise to get organised in advance.

Monday 11th

11:11 is often a magical time on the 11th day of the month, so you should think about arranging something special for this moment. It's a good idea to link this moment to your career and where you want to be in 2024. Try to make time for a social get-together this evening.

Tuesday 12th

Today's new moon highlights issues concerning your career and vocation. If you're looking for a job, apply for one; if you want to launch a new project, go for it. Take advantage of the dynamic, fast-paced energy over the next fortnight by focusing on your career and where you're heading in life.

Wednesday 13th

Mercury turns retrograde, and this means that it's not the best time to make major decisions about friendships or groups. Instead, it's better to pull back and wait for a few weeks. However, it is a good time to catch up with old friends and to put in some time to research your next steps.

Thursday 14th

You may be asked to step out of your routine to make time for a good friend today, especially if they've been caught out by Mercury turning retrograde. Provide the help they need and enjoy the opportunity to catch up.

Friday 15th

A social event may be cancelled or postponed today, or you might simply decide that you don't want to attend. Either way, you should welcome this extra time to yourself, especially if you're worn out or you want to get on top of your correspondence and chores.

Saturday 16th

This weekend's stars favour time alone rather than social shenanigans, and suggest that you should go on a retreat or enjoy a peaceful group event. Alternatively, you might choose to be quiet and switch off social media. Either way, take some time out to recharge your batteries.

Sunday 17th

If you're confused or unsure about what comes next, try not to overcommit yourself. You're likely to be the sort of person that sometimes gives too much or comes up with too many different options, and this can leave you without a sense of direction. Be kind to yourself now and rest when you need to.

Monday 18th

You may find that you're more interested in your friends and social life than work and chores today. Perhaps you're thinking about someone who pops up on your social media timeline. Follow any coincidences and memories and see where they lead you, especially if you're looking for love.

Tuesday 19th

You may be ready to take a step back from your work and career goals, especially if you want to focus on your personal goals instead. This is a lovely day to boost your image and confidence, so consider a trip to the hairdresser's or treat yourself to a new outfit.

Wednesday 20th

Your star sign is renowned for having a soft heart, so you're likely to care deeply about people and animals. However, it's important that you don't let someone talk you into focusing too much kindness on the world around you, especially if it comes at the expense of your own happiness.

Thursday 21st

One of the joys of this festive season might be the chance to rediscover old friends or get back in touch with someone you worked with years ago. Try to find time for anyone who reaches out. If you're booking a holiday, make sure you double-check everything and try to be flexible about your dates.

Friday 22nd

It's both the shortest day of the year and, for Pisces, one of the most sociable. The Sun moves into your friendship and group zone, so you might be at one of the biggest events of the year or heading off to meet up with your family. The bigger the event, the better.

Saturday 23rd

You may change your mind about your career or where you're heading next. However, it's important not to act rashly while Mercury remains retrograde, so take your time to think things through. If you feel compelled to contact someone you used to work with, you're in tune with your stars.

Sunday 24th

It's the perfect time to prioritise the important people in your life. You're more likely to be happy at home if you're surrounded by family or celebrating Christmas Eve with one of your oldest friends. It's not the best idea to be on your own, so look for comfort and connection.

Monday 25th

The moon is in your home and family zone, so being with loved ones will be the perfect way to spend Christmas Day. There may be a thrill of romance in the air, especially if you hear from a loved one who lives abroad or you're lucky enough to be enjoying a holiday romance in an exotic destination.

. . . .

Tuesday 26th

Try not to get involved in any talk about work or career plans today, as doing so might lead to an argument rather than a discussion. The same may be true if you're irritated by a family member's lack of ambition. It's not the best day to address any sensitive issues. Play some family games tonight.

Wednesday 27th

Today's full moon may be especially romantic for you, especially if you prioritise love and happiness and connect fully with your emotional nature. If you want to commit to something big, this is the ideal full moon to declare your intentions. Hugs and affection make the world a better place.

Thursday 28th

If you want to talk to someone about their plans, be prepared to listen rather than just telling them what you think they should do. If you're disillusioned about where you're heading and you would like things to happen faster, consider taking a punt and kickstarting a new work idea.

Friday 29th

If you're working over the next couple of days, it's likely to be a sociable and fun time. There's a friendly vibe, so you'll enjoy being around other people. It's a good weekend to help the people around you. In terms of your career, it may be that it's not what you know but who you know that counts right now.

Saturday 30th

Time management could go out the window today, especially if your plans have to change unexpectedly. Be adaptable and flexible, as these are two of the greatest traits of your star sign. A night spent with good friends is the perfect way to enjoy yourself now.

Sunday 31st

You have Jupiter, the planet of luck and good fortune, on your side today, so you might hear some good news or find that someone special in your life turns up unexpectedly. You'll be happiest on New Year's Eve if you're with the one you love. It's also a wonderful night to meet someone new.

Pisces

....

PEOPLE WHO SHARE
YOUR SIGN

PEOPLE WHO
SHARE YOUR SIGN

. . . .

No pinch can take the faraway sign of Pisces out of their dreamland. With their artistic flair, compassionate hearts and wonderful imaginations, Pisceans both inspire and heal. Whether it's sharing their visionary talents, like Alexander McQueen and Jenny Packham, or emotional lyrics, like Kurt Cobain and Johnny Cash, the gifts from Pisceans help to restore a sense of magic to the world. Discover which of these enchanting Pisceans share your birthday and see if you can spot the similarities between them.

20th February

Rihanna (1988), Miles Teller (1987), Trevor Noah (1984), Chelsea Peretti (1978), Kurt Cobain (1967), Cindy Crawford (1966), Walter Becker (1950), Ivana Trump (1949), Mitch McConnell (1942)

21st February

Sophie Turner (1996), Riyad Mahrez (1991), Ashley Greene (1987), Elliot Page (1987), Mélanie Laurent (1983), Jennifer Love Hewitt (1979), Jordan Peele (1979), Michael McIntyre (1976), Kelsey Grammar (1955), Alan Rickman (1946), Nina Simone (1933), Hubert de Givenchy (1927)

22nd February

Drew Barrymore (1975), James Blunt (1974), Jeri Ryan (1968), Steve Irwin (1962), Kyle MacLachlan (1959), Julie Walters (1950), Niki Lauda (1949), Robert Kardashian (1944), Bruce Forsyth (1928)

23rd February

Dakota Fanning (1994), Skylar Grey (1986), Andre Ward (1984), Aziz Ansari (1983), Emily Blunt (1983), Josh Gad (1981), Kelly Macdonald (1976), Daymond John (1969), Kristin Davis (1965), W. E. B. Du Bois (1868)

24th February

Earl Sweatshirt (1994), O'Shea Jackson Jr. (1991), Priscilla Chan (1985), Floyd Mayweather (1977), Bonnie Somerville (1974), Billy Zane (1966), Steve Jobs (1955), Phil Knight (1938)

25th February

Eugenie Bouchard (1994), Rashida Jones (1976), Chelsea Handler (1975), Sean Astin (1971), Téa Leoni (1966), George Harrison (1943), Anthony Burgess (1917), Pierre-Auguste Renoir (1841)

26th February

CL (1991), Charley Webb (1988), Teresa Palmer (1986), Erykah Badu (1971), Max Martin (1971), Michael Bolton (1953), Johnny Cash (1932), William Cody (1846), Victor Hugo (1802), Christopher Marlowe (1564)

27th February

Lindsey Morgan (1990), JWoww (1986), Kate Mara (1983), Josh Groban (1981), Chelsea Clinton (1980), Peter Andre (1973), Li Bingbing (1973), Derren Brown (1971), Timothy Spall (1957), Elizabeth Taylor (1932), John Steinbeck (1902)

143

28th February

Sarah Bolger (1991), Olivia Palermo (1986), Karolína Kurková (1984), Natalia Vodianova (1982), Ali Larter (1976), Amanda Abbington (1974), Ainsley Harriott (1957), Paul Krugman (1953), Bernadette Peters (1948), Frank Gehry (1929)

29th February

Jessie T. Usher (1992), Mark Foster (1984), Ja Rule (1976), Pedro Sánchez, Spanish Prime Minister (1972), Dennis Farina (1944), Gioachino Rossini (1792)

1st March

Justin Bieber (1994), Kesha (1987), Lupita Nyong'o (1983), Jensen Ackles (1978), Javier Bardem (1969), Paul Hollywood (1966), Zack Snyder (1966), Ron Howard (1954), Harry Belafonte (1927), Frédéric Chopin (1810)

2nd March

Becky G (1997), Nathalie Emmanuel (1989), Bryce Dallas Howard (1981), Rebel Wilson (1980), Chris Martin (1977), Alexander Armstrong (1970), Daniel Craig (1968), Jon Bon Jovi (1962), Karen Carpenter (1950), Lou Reed (1942), Dr. Theodor Seuss (1904)

3rd March

Camila Cabello (1997), Jessica Biel (1982), Ronan Keating (1977), Alison King (1973), Julie Bowen (1970), Ira Glass (1959), Miranda Richardson (1958), Zico (1953), Alexander Graham Bell (1847)

4th March

Brooklyn Beckham (1999), Bobbi Kristina Brown (1993), Draymond Green (1990), Whitney Port (1985), Chaz Bono (1969), Patsy Kensit (1968), Sam Taylor-Johnson (1967), Tim Vine (1967), Khaled Hosseini (1965), Patricia Heaton (1958), Catherine O'Hara (1954), Shakin' Stevens (1948)

5th March

Madison Beer (1999), Sterling Knight (1989), Dan Carter (1982), Hanna Alström (1981), Jolene Blalock (1975), Eva Mendes (1974), John Frusciante (1970), Lisa Robin Kelly (1970), Talia Balsam (1959), Esther Hicks (1948)

6th March

Tyler, the Creator (1991), Agnieszka Radwańska (1989), Shaquille O'Neal (1972), Connie Britton (1967), Rob Reiner (1947), David Gilmour (1946), Valentina Tereshkova (1937), Gabriel García Márquez (1927), Michelangelo (1475)

7th March

Laura Prepon (1980), Jenna Fischer (1974), Matthew Vaughn (1971), Rachel Weisz (1970), Wanda Sykes (1964), E. L. James (1963), Bryan Cranston (1956), Piet Mondrian (1872)

8th March

Stephanie Davis (1993), Petra Kvitová (1990), Kat Von D (1982), James Van Der Beek (1977), Freddie Prinze Jr. (1976), Florentino Pérez, (1947), Randy Meisner (1946)

9th March

YG (1990), Bow Wow (1987), Brittany Snow (1986), Matthew Gray Gubler (1980), Oscar Isaac (1979), Juliette Binoche (1964), Bobby Fischer (1943), Yuri Gagarin (1934)

10th March

Belinda Benic (1997), Emily Osment (1992), Ivan Rakitic (1988), Olivia Wilde (1984), Carrie Underwood (1983), Samuel Eto'o (1981), Timbaland (1972), Jon Hamm (1971), Sharon Stone (1958), Chuck Norris (1940)

11th March

Thora Birch (1982), LeToya Luckett (1981), Benji Madden (1979), Joel Madden (1979), Didier Drogba (1978), Johnny Knoxville (1971), Terrence Howard (1969), Jenny Packham (1965), Alex Kingston (1963)

12th March

Christina Grimmie (1994), Stromae (1985), Jaimie Alexander (1984), Pete Doherty (1979), Aaron Eckhart (1968), James Taylor (1948), Liza Minnelli (1946), Jack Kerouac (1922)

13th March

Jordyn Jones (2000), Mikaela Shiffrin (1995), Kaya Scodelario (1992), Tristan Thompson (1991), Common (1972), Jorge Sampaoli (1960), Dana Delany (1956), William H. Macy (1950)

14th March

Simone Biles (1997), Stephen Curry (1988), Jamie Bell (1986), Taylor Hanson (1983), Chris Klein (1979), Brian Quinn (1976), Megan Follows (1968), Billy Crystal (1948), Michael Caine (1933), Quincy Jones (1933), Albert Einstein (1879)

15th March

Paul Pogba (1993), Lil Dicky (1988), Jai Courtney (1986), Kellan Lutz (1985), Eva Longoria (1975), will.i.am (1975), Bret Michaels (1963), Fabio Lanzoni (1959), Mike Love (1941), Ruth Bader Ginsburg (1933), Gerda Wegener (1886)

16th March

Wolfgang Van Halen (1991), Theo Walcott (1989), Jhené Aiko (1988), Alexandra Daddario (1986), Danny Brown (1981), Brooke Burns (1978), Sophie Hunter (1978), Alan Tudyk (1971), Lauren Graham (1967), Flavor Flav (1959), Victor Garber (1949), Jerry Lewis (1926)

17th March

John Boyega (1992), Hozier (1990), Grimes (1988), Rob Kardashian (1987), Edin Džeko (1986), Coco Austin (1979), Brittany Daniel (1976), Alexander McQueen (1969), Billy Corgan (1967), Rob Lowe (1964), Gary Sinise (1955), Kurt Russell (1951), Pattie Boyd (1944), Nat King Cole (1919)

18th March

Lily Collins (1989), Danneel Ackles (1979), Adam Levine (1979), Alex Jones (1977), Emma Willis (1976), Queen Latifah (1970), Peter Jones (1966), Vanessa Williams (1963), Grover Cleveland, U.S. President (1837)

19th March

Héctor Bellerín (1995), Garrett Clayton (1991), AJ Lee (1987), Bianca Balti (1984), Eduardo Saverin (1982), Kolo Touré (1981), Bruce Willis (1955), Glenn Close (1947), Ursula Andress (1936), David Livingstone (1813)

20th March

Marcos Rojo (1990), Ruby Rose (1986), iJustine (1984), Fernando Torres (1984), Freema Agyeman (1979), Chester Bennington (1976), Michael Rapaport (1970), Kathy Ireland (1963), David Thewlis (1963), Holly Hunter (1958), Spike Lee (1957), Douglas Tompkins (1943), Fred Rogers (1928), B. F. Skinner (1904)